VOL I.

PSYCHOLOGY

BY

ANNIE BESANT

ISBN: 978-1-63923-036-5

Printed: March 2023

Published and Distributed By:
Lushena Books
607 Country Club Drive, Unit E
Bensenville, IL 60106
www.lushenabks.com

ISBN: 978-1-63923-036-5

CONTENTS

A Word on Man
His Nature and His Powers

A Lecture delivered on board the "Kaisar-i-Hind," in the Red Sea, Oct. 30th, 1893.

(Reported.)

The last time I spoke to you I took a very large subject, which I was obliged to treat very roughly. To-night I have selected a smaller subject, although still a large one, and shall be able therefore to treat it a little more fully. I propose to put before you what the Esoteric Philosophy teaches concerning man: man's nature and man's powers, his possibilities in the future, as well as his state in the present. May I say in opening what I have to put to you, that I am simply laying before you that which I have been taught, and which I have to a considerable extent verified by my own personal experiment, so that it has become to me a matter of knowledge? I, however, only put it to you as a matter of reasonable hypothesis. I do not pretend to dictate to you your opinions; I do not pretend to formulate for you what you shall think, or what you shall reject. On each of you the

responsibility of forming his own thought; on each
of you the responsibility of accepting or rejecting, as
your own reason, your conscience and your judgment may decide. All that the speaker can do, or has
the right to do, is to put the truth as he sees it, leaving it to each individual to accept or to reject, the
right and the duty being on each, and not on the
one who speaks.

With regard to man, there is a fundamental difference in the conception of man as he is looked at in the
East and in the West. According to the Esoteric
Philosophy man is regarded essentially as a soul.
What he may have of instruments which that soul
employs, what bodies he may clothe himself in, what
special forms he may adopt—all that is matter which
changes in time and space. As you may read in the
Brihad Aranyaka Upanishad: "As a goldsmith, taking a piece of gold, forms another shape . . . so
throwing off this body . . . the soul forms a shape."
And so the man is the soul, the soul that lives to
gather experience, that lives to subjugate external
nature, that lives to unite itself with the Divine
Spirit from whence it sprang; and as regards the
soul's bodies, those differ as evolution proceeds, and
the soul moulds them century after century into the
fuller and more perfect expression of itself. But in
the West, man is far more identified with his outer
form; he identifies himself with his body and with

his mind. To us the soul stands above body and mind, using both as instruments, whereas in the West, people think of themselves as consisting of body and of mind; and the things that interest them are the things that affect the body, while the mind, they think, is practically their master, and they never dream of mastering their own thoughts and being ruler of their own intellectual as well as of their own physical domain.

In order that these distinctions may be understood, let us sketch the different "principles," as they are sometimes called—"states of consciousness," as they are called at other times—which make up man when you take him completely, as man physical, man psychical and man spiritual. Those are the three great divisions accepted, let me say in passing, by Christianity as much as by other religions. For you find St. Paul speaking of a man "as body, soul and spirit." I know that in popular Christianity the distinction between soul and spirit has very largely been lost. But that is not so in Christian philosophy. If you take the writings of the great thinkers of Christendom, those who have dealt with religion scientifically and philosophically, you will find they follow the lines laid down by the great Christian Apostle, and regard man as a triple and not only as a dual entity. Now the body which belongs to the man, which is a physical garment as we say, is a very changing and a

very illusory thing, as I said to you the other night—
changing continually from moment to moment, and
from year to year; so that if you turn to any modern
book on physiology you will find that every minute
particle of your body changes absolutely and completely in the space of seven years, that not a fragment of it you had seven years ago is yours to-day.
Not only so. In the later investigations of physiology
you will find it recognised in the West, that a great
part, at least, of the body, is made up of minute lives,
microbes as they are called; and whenever men of
science are searching after the cause of disease, they
are on the track of some particular microbe, and it has
become one of their favourite recreations to cultivate
the microbe and improve him, so that he may become
less dangerous when he falls upon any particular
body. In this, Western science is on the track of a
great truth, and as far as it goes, it speaks rightly in
the fact that these microbes enter into the composition
of the human body. It might go further: it might
say that the whole body is made up of nothing else
but microbes and more minute creatures still, so that
the whole body of man is composed of tiny lives, lives
each with its own independent existence, coming into
the body and going out of it, taking while in the body
the stamp of the individual man, of which, for a time,
it forms a part. So that our bodies are like hosts of
these tiny visitors, and each of us stamps on those

particles of the body his own physical, and to a great
extent, his mental, moral and emotional characteristics. Out of the great reservoir of nature, there pour
through us these streams of tiny lives; and each,
while it remains in our keeping, receives our stamp
and then passes on to form·part of some other body—
vegetable, mineral, animal, human, as the case may
be. So that even physically we become the creators
of the world in which we live. Even physically,
the world as it surrounds us, is made up of that which
we contribute, and is modified and changed according
to the character of these constant contributions that
we make. Into our body flow the tiny lives. There we
feed them, poison them or purify them, pollute them
or cleanse them, as the case may be. By our food and
by our living, we modify these tiny particles which
are a passing part of ourselves; and then we send
them out to affect others—to make part of the bodies of
other people, to make part of the physical nature
around us, modifying them according to the fashion
in which'we are living ourselves. This is the physical
basis of the brotherhood of all that lives. And there
is nothing that lives not. So that this constant interaction throws on each a responsibility, gives to·each
the responsibility of this creative power, of this
transmuting and modifying influence. One by one we
change each other's lives physically, day by day we
affect each other's health mentally as well as morally.

Sometimes it is said that the man who is evil in his living, as the drunkard, is only his own enemy. It is not so. He is the enemy of everything that surrounds him, of every life that comes in contact with his own. The terrible curse of the drunkard is that all these tiny lives are sent out from him, poisoned with alcohol, to fall on the bodies of other men, women and children, carrying with them the poison that he has infused into them, and making him a focus of evil to all among whom he lives. Thus, learning what the physical body is, the Esoteric Philosophy makes us careful in our physical life. It carries on this sense of responsibility into the common actions, common thoughts of everyday and ordinary life, so that self-restraint in the body as well as in the mind, should be the note of the life of every true Theosophist.

Let me pass from the body to the next stage in man, that astral body to which I alluded the other night. Really the astral body should come first in our thought, for it is the stable matrix or mould, into which all of these tiny physical lives pass, and out of which they pass again, the stable part of man which preserves the form, only slowly and gradually modified, which is more directly acted upon by the mind than the physical molecules, which affects the physical molecules in their arrangement, in that as you alter the matrix, these physical molecules must take on the form of the mould into which they run. This astral body of astral matter envelopes every physical molecule, but spreads out around the body, making a kind of atmosphere around each of us, extending some few feet away on every side, so that a clairvoyant looking at the body, sees the physical body surrounded by what is called an aura, that is, a vibrating mass of delicate matter, visible to anyone who is sensitive under special conditions, but visible normally to the clairvoyant, and differing in appearance according to the state of health, physical, psychical or mental, of the person whom it concerns. Now, that aura or atmosphere surrounding the body, which is in a sense an expression of astral matter, is very closely connected with the mind; it is very easily affected by the mind of the person to whom it belongs, and also by the minds of others. These magnetic atmospheres that surround us (for in astral matter all magnetic forces play) bring us into contact one with the other, so that we affect each other unconsciously, as we sometimes say. Have you never felt on meeting a person for the first time an attraction or a repulsion which had nothing in it of intellectual judgment, nothing in it of previous knowledge or experience? You like a person—you cannot tell why; you dislike another—you have no reason for your dislike. Esoteric Philosophy explains to you the very simple reason that causes these strange antipathies and attractions. It is that every human being has his own rate of vibration, the vibration of this astral matter,

so that it is always quivering backwards and forwards.
It is one of the characteristics of this ethereal matter
to be thrown easily into waves; and just as light is
nothing more than waves of ether set in very rapid
motion by a rapidly vibrating body, which we call
luminous, because of the effect it has upon the eye, so
this ethereal matter, which is part of our own bodies,
is thrown into waves of definite length and definite
frequency; and these vibrate always in and around
us, and are part of ourselves, modified by our own
characteristics. Just as striking two strings on a
piano, you may have either harmony or discord, according to the length of the sound-waves set up by
these vibrating strings, so you may have either harmony or discord, according to the length of the sound-
waves set up by these vibrating strings, so you may
have either harmony or discord between the vibrating
auras of two different people; and if the vibrations
fall into harmony—that is, if they bear a certain
definite relation of wave length to each other—there
is an attraction between the two: whereas, if they
bear a different relation, you get discord—that is,
friction and jangle, and you are repelled without
understanding the reason.

It is this astral body and astral atmosphere which
are the medium for all magnetic phenomena. All the
effects we produce upon each other are modified by
this astral atmosphere. All the effects that deal with

emotions and passions, with all those sides of the human character which are of the nature of emotion, come to us by means of these astral vibrations.

Have you ever tried to think what oratory is? It does not lie in the words that are spoken; it does not lie in the thought that is behind the words. You might take in cold blood the most eloquent passage of some great oration, and read it calmly without any movement of the emotions, without any sense of passion or of vibrating enthusiasm in you. If you hear it spoken, it is different. Why? It is because the thought of the speaker, working on his own astral atmosphere, throws that into vehement vibrations— vibrations of love or of hatred, passion or pity—vibrations of great enthusiasm; and then these vibrations of his throwing the whole ether around him into wave motion, these waves strike person after person, making their own atmosphere vibrate, and then from one to another there flies the contagion until the whole crowd is moved as by a single impulse and a single will.

These are all results of this second part of man's nature, this astral atmosphere that penetrates and surrounds him, by means of which the mind works on physical matter. And not only in this fashion, but in many forms of nervous disease, in those strange crises of panic, in those often puzzling attacks of hysterical affection that rush through a whole hospital. There you have set up these vibrations in the astral atmosphere communicated from patient to patient, and bringing about nervous crises in the physical body which they control.

With regard to this astral body and atmosphere, many investigations are being made by modern science, and many of our acutest thinkers are beginning to realise that it is necessary to postulate such a nature in man in order to explain many of the obscurer phenomena, to which so much of our modern thought is directed. Into this part of man's nature fall all the phenomena of trance, all the lower phenomena of mesmerism, and many of the phenomena of hypnotism. Although mind comes into mesmeric and hypnotic phenomena, it works on the astral body of the person who is subject to the influence, and by producing effects in the astral body, brings about results in the physical. Psychologists in the West—men like Sidgwick, Sully, Bain, and many another of our leading writers on psychology —have found that they cannot understand the workings of consciousness if they only study it in its waking state; that is, if they only study the mind as we know it in our waking hours, they meet with phenomena that are quite inexplicable, and they have begun to study sleep-consciousness—a very bad name for it, but apparently there is no better, at present, in the English tongue—in order the better to understand the phenomena shown by the mind in its waking state. This sleep-consciousness includes all conditions of trance. There is this advantage of the trance condition—you can produce it at will; and every scientist will tell you that if he wants to gain exact facts, he needs to control his experiments, and to shut out what he does not want, to include only the conditions which he desires in order that he may make his experiments. The moment he can produce these special conditions, he can work out all the facts he is in search of with less liability to error than would otherwise occur. By artificially inducing trance, human consciousness can be studied in a fashion which is normally impossible; trance is produced sometimes by drugs, sometimes by mesmeric passes—that is, by the action of the mind and the will upon another, sometimes by hypnotism—that is, by using a mechanical stimulus like a revolving mirror or electric light (there are many ways of doing it)—fatiguing the external sense, so that the fatigue leads to paralysis of the cells of the nerve, and that paralysis is propagated backwards to the brain, producing ultimately a state of brain fatigue, brain paralysis, in fact, a state of coma. In these fashions, man may be thrown into these abnormal states of consciousness, and studied when consciousness is working in this particular state instead of in the normal condition. In hypnotism these results are brought about mechanically. Mr. Braid, who first started these hypnotic experiments, brought them about by producing what he called a convergent stabismus. That is only a six-syllabled way of saying "a squint"; but sometimes the scientific mind likes to speak in six syllables rather than in one, because it produces a certain sense of dignity which impresses the unscientific and thoughtless. Really what he did, was to make the patient squint upwards by putting an object slightly above the eyes so that they had to converge in looking at it. In that way he fatigued very seriously the nervous elements as well as the muscles of the eye; and so the patient passed into a state of sleep or trance, from which Mr. Braid was able to obtain what are known as hypnotic phenomena. The older phenomena of mesmerism were brought about in a different way, by a person who was able to concentrate his will and his own magnetic force, throwing that force with all the strength of concentrated will on the person he desired to affect. He worked directly on the astral body by means of mental action; whereas the hypnotist works on the astral body by way of the physical, and so produces the bad physical effect, that by making artificial paralysis he fatigues the nerve and sets up unhealthy vibrations which tend to repeat themselves. Charcot always preferred to work on hysterical people, people with a tendency to epilepsy and other forms of mental disease; those were the people most easily affected. He did not so much try to cure them, as to find out what results he could obtain from them, and the results were a further shattering of the nervous system as well as some exceedingly psychical facts; but these facts were largely obtained at the cost of the physical destruction of human beings, a thing utterly antagonistic to all morality, and which ought to be condemned as a kind of human vivisection, even more wicked and more cruel than the vivisection of the lower animals. The results thus obtained you may read in many books that have been published. I shall only take a few samples to show the way in which by means of the astral the mind may work upon the physical body and so bring about results which will lead us on to our next part, the working of mind in forming images, and so later in moulding physical matter at its own will.

Take an ordinary hypnotic or mesmeric experiment. I should prefer mesmerism. Personally, I do not now use any of these experiments (I used to do them in my early days of investigation, before I knew the harm I might work), as I think on the whole they are mischievous. A person is thrown into a trance, and in that state he is told, say, that on his hand at a certain hour in the day will appear symptoms of a burn, that the skin will get red, that pain

will be felt, that a wound will appear like a wound
formed by a red-hot poker, and that all the symptoms, inflammatory and other, of a burn will be
present. He awakes out of the trance, and so far as
you are able to discover he knows nothing of what
has occurred during that time. The hour arrives
which has been fixed for this appearance; the skin
begins to redden and pain is felt. The patient does
not understand what is happening, but he is conscious that he is suffering pain. The symptoms become more acute; the skin gradually assumes an appearance which it would assume if touched by a
poker, and you have a burn produced, not by external lesion, but by the action of mind, the mind of
the operator working through the astral body of the
patient, setting up there the image of a burn which
then reproduces itself on the physical molecules,
which, as I explained before, are shaped and
moulded by the astral matrix in which they are em-
bedded. If, when in Paris, you go to the *Salpétrière,*
you can see a number of photographs which have
been taken of burns which have thus been produced
on the bodies of patients, and you may examine the
doctors who have produced these lesions and without
external means have caused external injury.

This throws strong light on some so-called miracles.
Where you have the production of what have been
called the sacred stigmata—that is, the appearance

on the hands and feet of the wounds of the Passion
of Jesus—you are not face to face with a fraud, as
many Protestants are apt to think, when dealing
with a Roman Catholic miracle. You are not face to
face with a case of deliberate self-deception any more
than a wilful deception of others. You are simply
face to face with hypnotic phenomena produced in
highly nervous subjects—such, say, as secluded
monks or nuns who have their minds fixed constantly
on one idea, who very often remain for hours in a
single position with eyes upturned towards the Crucifix—in that very position in which Braid used to
bring on his hypnotic trance. So are really produced
these marks upon the physical body, which by those
who believe them to be miraculous are looked on as
endorsing a particular form of faith, while by those
who hold another form of Christianity, they are regarded as deliberate and wicked frauds. They are
neither the one nor the other. Like all miracles they
are reducible under law; for a miracle is only the
working of a law unknown to the people amongst
whom the phenomenon occurs, and they, because
they do not understand it, at once jump to the
"supernatural," forgetting that, as the Divine is the
source of all, there can be nothing which is not
natural—there can be nothing outside and beyond
the divine nature and the divine will. Take, then,
that class of phenomena as interesting physically—

interesting as showing that you can produce physical results without what we call a physical cause—a thing which fifty years ago science would have said was impossible, which fifty years ago would have been denounced as fraud, as it was denounced when brought about a hundred years ago by a man like Mesmer. Orthodox science denounced him as a charlatan and a rogue. The century that followed has justified Mesmer, and has made some of us fairly indifferent when science calls out "fraud" about other phenomena which we know to be as real and as natural as those which were denounced as fraudulent by the science of the eighteenth century, and are boasted of as modern triumphs by the science of the nineteenth. These, however, are the least interesting of such phenomena. Far more interesting are the mental workings on the mind of the patient —placing before him thought images produced in the mind of the operator, and so enabling him to see as an image that which only exists as thought in the mind of the controller.

But before referring to some of these experiments, let me give you an explanation from the standpoint of the philosophy I am trying to explain. I have spoken of the soul as the man. That soul when it works through astral matter on the brain is known as mind, for the mind is the lower manifestation of the soul—it is the soul embodied and active in the

body, not the soul in its own nature, not the soul in
its own sphere, not the soul which used mind as
well as body as instrument, but only the soul as it
is seen and manifested in the brain—intellect, reason,
judgment, memory: all those characteristics of the
mind are qualities of the soul as the soul works
through the brain. In its own sphere it works in
matter of a much subtler kind, and there each
thought is a thing. Every thought is a form; every
thought has its shape in the subtle matter which is
the matter of the soul-sphere. But when that shape
is to make itself manifest to others who are living
in the body, it must clothe itself in astral matter to
begin with, and take a shape in which, in the trance
or clairvoyant shape, it can be seen as a form; then
it may be projected further into physical manifestation. With that I will deal in a moment.
Amongst those physical manifestations are some of
the phenomena which have caused so much puzzle-
ment in connection with the Theosophical Society in
the minds of many both in the East and the West.

Let me take, then, with that brief explanation,
the workings of the soul through the mind, the
working of the mind on astral matter, and the proofs
of it that you may obtain through mesmeric and
hypnotic phenomena. Suppose you take a sheet of
plain paper and throw your patient into a mesmeric
trance. On that paper place a card smaller than

the paper and then trace round it with a little bit
of wood an outline of the card. Say to the person
who is in trance, "I will draw a line round the
card, and you can see it." Then put the paper and
the card away, and wake the person out of the
trance. Apparently he will be quite normal, like you
or me. Give him, then, half-a-dozen bits of blank
paper, amongst which is the paper on which this
imaginary line has been drawn round the edge of
the card, and ask him if on any of these bits of
paper he sees any figure. He will pass them over one
by one, and when he comes to the paper on which
this line has been drawn by the wood, he will say—
"On this there is an oblong traced." In order to be
sure that he sees it, ask him to fold the paper along
the line he sees, and he will fold it along these
"imaginary" lines that you cannot see. Then bring
the card and place it on the folded paper, and you
will find that he has folded along invisible lines so
that he has the exact size of the card round which
this "imaginary" line was traced, showing you that
he sees this image that has been formed, and that it
persists for him, his faculties having been thrown
into this clairvoyant state.

Take another case rather more complicated. Here
you want considerable concentration of will on the
part of the operator. On a blank piece of paper
throw an image. Take, for example, a watch. If

you look at the watch it conveys a very definite
image to your mind. Are you able in thought to
project such an image on the piece of paper so that
you can see it with the mind? That is what is called
visualising it. Some have great power in doing it.
Every artist has the power to some extent. Every
person can obtain it if he chooses to train his will
and concentrate. You can thus produce to your own
mind a clear image, so that if you shut your eyes you
can see the watch in thought. That is the condition
of success in an experiment of this kind. Suppose I
have my patient: in my thought I throw an image of
the watch on the paper, that is, I fix my mind on
the paper, and I see on it in my own thought an
image of the watch. I need not speak a word, I
need not make any sign or touch the patient; there
shall be no contact between him and me; I will remain silent, and affect him by nothing except my
mind. He shall then be awakened out of the trance.
Some one else shall give him the bits of paper, so
that there may not even be contact between my
touch of the paper and his touch. Presently, looking over the bits of paper, he will come to the one
on which my thought has made the image of the
watch, and say, "Here is a watch." Ask him to
describe it and he will describe it. Take it away,
remove it to a distance until the outline grows dim,
and he will say, "I cannot see it clearly." Now give

him an opera glass and the image will be recovered. Give him finally a pencil and ask him to trace over the lines of the picture he sees, and he will draw on that apparently blank paper the picture that you have made by your mind. What has happened?

The mind has in astral matter made the image by the force of its own thought, and that is visible to the person in the clairvoyant state. His astral body, which is active, vibrates in answer to it, and so by an inner sense he is able to see it. That is then transmitted to the physical eye, and he sees that which to the eye not thus influenced does not exist. But what is thus seen must exist, or it could not be visible under any conditions. On these matters Professor Lodge is making some interesting investigations. He has convinced himself that thought can pass from brain to brain by means of an idea being conveyed without any word or written expression at all. In all those experiments, case after case may be found by which you may convince yourselves of the reality that thought—ideation— gives birth to form. But this may carry us very far. I have said that concentrated thought is necessary for such exact experiments, but it is not necessary for affecting to some extent the minds of others, which are all in nature like our own. Very concentrated thought is necessary to produce an astral image that another can see; comparatively slight thought is wanted to produce an image that another may receive in the mind. And so you come to thought-transference, another of man's powers familiar to every student of Theosophy, and now being investigated by modern science.

Before taking that, let me take the last stage of this production of images, which I said was connected with some of the phenomena which have caused so much curiosity and wonder and accusations of fraud in connection, especially, with Madame Blavatsky, the greatest wonder-worker of our time. It is a simple enough thing, this production of external material forms by a person who has trained the mind and the will. That means, of course, that the soul is sufficiently developed to be able to use the mind as an instrument—that which is thought to be impossible, I am afraid, in the Western world. What happens is this. The soul in its own sphere strongly thinks, and produces an image. That mind-image, generated by the soul, is thrown. down into the ordinary mind working in connection with astral matter. Then, into that mind-image is built astral matter—the molecules of astral matter—so that, as in the former case, it would become visible to the clairvoyant. But a stage further is possible. Out of the atmosphere in which, in minute division, as you know, exists physical matter, minute particles of carbon, for instance, in the carbonic acid around us—those particles taken up by the plant and built into its own tissues—those tiny particles of solid matter are precipitated by means of a magnetic current into the form which has thus been produced by the action of mind on the astral matter. And thus a physical object is produced. The commonest form of this is the precipitation of writing. All that is necessary is that you should be able to think strongly each letter that you want to produce. You must make an image of the letter; you must then produce an astral image of that letter, so that, say, your letter A would exist in an astral form, held together by strong concentrated will. Then into that astral mould by a magnetic current, as easy to manipulate as the magnetic and galvanic currents used by your electricians when they precipitate silver from a solution on to the article they desire to plate—by quite as simple a process there is cast down out of the atmosphere the minute material particles which in their aggregation become visible: and then your letter A appears as precipitated on the paper. That is a description, stage by stage, of the production of precipitated writing. There is nothing miraculous about it; it is a simple process, as simple as any electric message, which, as you know, may be produced by writing on a tape by alternating currents which produce, if you desire, a facsimile of the writing of the operator at the other end. The difference between the working of the adept and the working of the electrician, is that the electrician wants an apparatus—a battery and a wire—to produce his result; while the adept uses the brain as his battery and wire. For the human brain, as one of these adepts has told us, is a most marvellous generator of force, a most wonderful transmuter of mental into physical and physical into mental forces. There takes place the great alchemy of nature, and it can be governed by a purified and concentrated will. If you ask me, "Can I do it?" I reply, "No, you cannot, because you have not trained yourself." Will you pardon me if I say what sounds very rude, that very few of you ever really think at all?

You drift. You do not think. You allow other people's thoughts to drift into your minds from the mental and astral world. The minds of most of us are nothing more than hotels into which drift the visiting thoughts that are in the mental atmosphere around: they come in for a bit, stay for a time, and drift out again—drifting in and out. So, men and women scarcely ever really think. Some minds are more like dustbins than even hotels, and they put up a sort of label, "Rubbish may be shot here," in the form of the most trivial and ridiculous novels, the most frivolous and childish newspapers. Yet men and women who spend hours in that fashion, wonder that they cannot manipulate the forces of the mind, or use the power of the will which needs years of training ere it becomes ductile and obedient to the soul.

If you want to see whether I am judging harshly, try and think for one minute of a single thing, and before you have thought of it for half a minute the mind will be off on some other subject. Try and think of a watch for a minute after I have stopped talking, and before you have thought of it a quarter of a minute, you will find yourself thinking, "What was it she said about it? how did she look when she said it? What was my neighbour doing at that particular moment?" Everything except the one thing of which you are trying to think. Then, perhaps, you will convince yourself, as I convinced myself by that very experiment, how very little power you have over the mind, how much you are at the mercy of outside thoughts, instead of using them as you yourselves please.

Or take another case. You have some great and pressing anxiety. You can do nothing at the moment; yet it will keep you awake all night. Why? Because it is your master instead of your mastering it. If you knew the life of the soul, if you understood the powers of the soul, you would never think of anything save that which you desired to think, and which you are using for some purpose. If you had coming on, say, some great lawsuit, and could do nothing to influence the result, you would not think of it until the time came: you would give your whole mind to other thought that was useful and spare yourself needless worry, which ages and kills far more than anything else.   Let me say in passing that the power to do it is one of the great experiences which have come to us in the knowledge of Eastern thought.   For, at least, we have among the Hindoos not great numbers who can do it, but great numbers who put before themselves that as an ideal, who know that it can be done, who realize the possibility, and who are standing witnesses of this reality of the higher life of the soul, and the possibility of rising above body and mind into the true life where all causes have their place.

But even our careless thinking gives rise to forms; and this is a practical point of importance to us. As we think we create forms, and those forms are according to the nature of our thought, good or bad according as the thought is evil and evil-working, or good and good-working.   The motive which underlies the thought governs the nature of the form to which we give birth; and that form when it passes out from us, passes into the astral world as a living thing, exists in that astral world influencing other people and forming part of the common stock of thoughts in the world. On this subject one of the great Eastern teachers has said:—

"Every thought of man upon being evolved passes into the inner world, and becomes an active entity by associating itself, coalescing we might term it, with an elemental—that is to say, with one of the semi-intelligent forces of the kingdom. It survives as an active intelligence— a creature of the mind's begetting—for a longer or shorter period proportionate with the original intensity of the cerebral action which generated it. Thus, a good thought is perpetuated as an active beneficent power, an evil one as a maleficent demon. And so man is continually peopling his current in space with a world of his own, crowded with the offsprings of his fancies, desires, impulses and passions; a current which re-acts upon any sensitive or nervous organization which comes in contact with it, in proportion to its dynamic intensity. The Buddhist calls this his 'Sandba'; the Hindu gives it the name of 'Karma:' "*

That is what you and I are doing all day long, every day and week and year of our lives—sending out these currents of thoughts, peopling the mental atmosphere with our own thoughts, good, bad, and indifferent, thoughts of love and hate, thoughts of

* *The Occult World*, A. P. Sinnett. Fifth Edition. Pp. 89-90.

kindness and bitterness, thoughts that bless and thoughts that curse mankind. Here is the creative region, here the greatest responsibility. I spoke of our power of physical creation: far more important is our power of moral creation; for as we give out thoughts, good or evil, so we affect our own and others' lives, so we build our present and our future, so we make the world of to-day and of to-morrow. What is the criminal? You and I think we can separate ourselves from the criminal, that we are so much better than he, not responsible for his crimes. Are you so sure? A criminal is a very receptive organism—passive, negative, with all the soil made by his own past thinking, that makes him easily attract and nourish every thought which is evil and cruel. But the soil will not bear bad fruit unless evil seed fall into it. How much of that evil seed do you and I contribute? Perhaps some passing thought of anger, conquered a moment after comes into the mind. That thought has gone out into the mental atmosphere, becoming a living thing, a force for evil. That force of anger going into the mental atmosphere of the criminal, falling into the soil prepared for it, will germinate as a seed germinates, and there it may grow, nourished by his own evil, into an anger which is murder, and is then condemned by the criminal law of man. In the juster law of the universe the generator of the angry thought shares the fault of the crime. Everyone who helps thus to pollute his brother is guilty of his brother's sin. So, also, with good thought. Every noble thought that we think goes out into the world as force for good, and passing into some mind, whose soil is full of all good impulses, is nourished there into heroic action, and so comes forth as noble deed. Our saints and martyrs, our heroes and our thinkers, are ours in mind as well as by virtue of our common humanity. Our best goes to their making; our noblest goes to their helping. They are ours as we have helped to form them, and every thought we think of good goes to the making of the saint.

Such, then, is some of the teaching of Esoteric Philosophy as regards man's nature and man's powers. Everyone of us has thus a share in the making of the world; everyone of us has thus a share in the building of the future. To-day all that surrounds us is the outcome of past thinking; to-morrow our environment shall be the resultant of our present thought. Law everywhere: law in the mental and moral world as in the physical; but man the creator of his own destiny—man the builder, the moulder, the master of the world.

That, then, is the message which to-night I have striven to bring to you; that the fragment of esoteric truth that I have tried to put before you. For thus it is that morality worked out in contact with philosophy finds its embodiment in life. Thus life becomes beautiful, life becomes strong, life becomes dignified, noble and serene. You and I as living souls have the future in our hands to model: ours the power, ours, therefore, the responsibility; for where the power is, there, also, lies the duty; and with the increased knowledge of power the duty and the responsibility increase.

Proofs of the
Existence of the Soul

A Lecture delivered in 1903 in India.

In all ages of the world, among all civilisations and all peoples, there has existed that ineradicable tendency of man which we find expressed in the words of a Roman, "Not all of me shall die." But that conviction is not in the ordinary sense of the word in itself a proof. It might be argued from, as found everywhere and at all times, as apparently being part of human nature; but when I use the word "proof or proofs of the existence of the soul," I do not mean to appeal to that intuition, nor to base my argument on that often expressed conviction.

I intend to try to lead you step by step along a line of thought which the materialist might begin upon, although he would lose his materialism ere advancing very far; and I want to show you that in dealing with the soul we can proceed from step to step by clear and logical argument, so that the most reasonable and logical of people may be led gradually to admit the existence of a soul; or, at least, we can carry them at first to this point, that the balance of argument is in favour of such an existence, and that undoubtedly something exists beyond the mind. What that something is, is to be investigated by a different method of study. And it is much, when we can take a materialist and show him that a line of thought and of experiment is open to him which will land him in a position which almost compels him to advance, places him at a point where he can hardly logically stop, and so makes at least a *prima facie* ground which he may take as a platform from which to go further, as offering a sufficiently reasonable hypothesis to encourage a still deeper investigation.

Let us for a moment consider the basis of the materialistic argument with regard to thought and brain. It is an argument which now is falling entirely out of scientific favour, but it held a very high ground in scientific favour some five and twenty years ago; and at that time you could take up writer after writer amongst the respected scientists of the world, and you would be led by the whole tenor of their argument to conclude that, although they did not say so in so many words, thought was really the product, the result, of matter. Professor

Tyndall in that famous Belfast address, when he was dealing with matter and mind, said, as you may remember, that science would probably have entirely to recast its conceptions of matter; and that is most certainly a true prophecy. Since the Belfast address was delivered science has changed its conception of matter. It no longer gives to it the very narrow definition that it used to give in the days, say, of the youth of many of us. We find that nowadays matter is recognized as existing under conditions that five and twenty years ago would have been regarded as excluding the word "material," or as making it inapplicable.

Now, the old argument used to run, if I may just hastily go over it—for it was very familiar to me in the earlier days of my own thinking—that thought was directly produced by the action of the gray matter of the brain; that wherever such matter was found, thought was found in connection with it; that wherever it was not found, thought was absent; and that it was even possible to trace a quantitative relation between the amount of gray matter and the power of thought. Not only was this put in in a general way, but it was worked out with extreme care. You remember the old line along which the development of thought was traced in the growing child; how it was said that if you took a child's brain, the thought it could produce was infantile in its character; that as the brain developed into boyhood, thought grew stronger; that as the boy grew into a man, thought grew more powerful, more subtle; that as the man reached maturity the thought ripened with the growing maturity of the man; that if at any stage of the man's life the brain were injured, then the thought was changed in its character; that if the supply of blood were injured, say by any intoxicating liquor, then the thought became confused with the confused state of the brain; that if you found fever, so that the blood was in a bad condition, you had delirium affecting the thought; that if a bit of the skull-pan pressed on the brain, at once thought entirely either changed or disappeared, whereas, when you again lifted that piece of broken bone, thought returned. As the man grew old, thought weakened. When the brain began to decay, thought entirely vanished. If one little piece of the brain was eaten away, the faculty of the mind that expressed itself through that part of the brain disappeared. And then the argument was triumphantly summed up. If thought grows and increases and ripens with the growth and the increase and the ripening of the brain, if it varies with brain conditions, if it vanishes when the brain is seriously injured, if it grows weaker with the weakening of the brain, if as the brain decays thought power disappears, can we venture to say that when the brain falls to pieces after death, thought rises triumphant from its ruins and exists in strength and in majesty?

And the argument was a very strong argument, exceedingly strong to anyone who was accustomed to reason from point to point and to follow wherever the process of reasoning led. But the whole of that argument was based on induction. A conclusion can be reached by inductive logic, but there is always one difficulty in connection with any such argument. You must be sure that in any induction the whole of the facts are before you, for one fact omitted from your basis vitiates the whole of your conclusion. If one thing is left out, the whole superstructure falls; and always the weakness of the inductive argument is the possibility of some one fact having been overlooked. Unless you are sure that you know everything in the universe of discourse, inductive logic does not lead you to a certain and final conclusion.

Now, it was by the discovery of facts which were not included in that famous inductive argument, that the whole superstructure fell to pieces. One fact alone would have been enough, but instead of one, hundreds have come to the front. In any argument, which is based on the constant relation between two things, that constant relation must be shown to exist; and if you can get those same two things moving in an opposite direction, varying inversely, then what becomes of your argument? Now that is exactly what has happened in connection with the argument based on brain and thought and their constantly varying together. It has been found that they do not constantly vary together, and still more that they sometimes vary inversely; that is, that you may get a condition where the brain is partially paralysed, but where the thought is very much more active than when it was working in the brain.

Now, in these first steps of my argument I am not going to prove the soul, but I am going to prove that consciousness may exist apart from a physical organism; for it is that which needs to be proved first before a materialist will listen to you at all. There is no good talking about the soul as long as any person is of the opinion that thought is only the product of the brain—to use Carl Vogt's expression —as bile is the product of the liver. So long as a person holds that position, as some people do, you must shake him out of it by facts that he will recognise before you can begin to talk about the soul; and as every one agrees that the soul is connected with consciousness, if we can show that consciousness exists apart from that constant relation between brain and thought, we shall have made our first step out of materialism, and then we shall feel free to go further on in tracing the nature of this consciousness.

Now, speaking generally, a mass of mesmeric and hypnotic experiments put it beyond the possibility of challenge that intelligence can work when the brain is paralysed.

I prefer in dealing with this question not to take experiments which rest on the evidence of people who might be regarded as people to be challenged, because they are looked on more or less as "cranks," like Theosophists. I had rather take some good scientific man, a materialist, to begin with, because his evidence is so much more satisfactory to his fellow materialists. Always, if you can, get your opponent to prove your case; to prove your own case out of the mouth of your opponent's witness is supposed to be a triumph, I understand, in legal procedure. I shall therefore summon into my witness box some of the doctors in Paris who are materialists—who call themselves so; I am not calling them names—but who are utterly unable to account for the results that they have themselves obtained. Quite honestly they say that they do not put forward a theory; they simply record the facts that they have observed—a perfectly sound and proper position and a very useful one to take up.

Now, amongst their observations—for I have not time to dwell on them long—we find this: They have

invented an apparatus which tests the physical condition of the beating of the heart, etc., while the
patient is in the hypnotic state. They have some admirable instruments by which they can measure
exactly the beating of the heart, the movement of
the lungs, the contraction of the muscles, and so
on. So that by means of this apparatus they can
get a perfectly accurate record of the physical conditions of the person under observation, a quite
necessary thing when you want to proceed slowly
from step to step. The instrument that they generally use is one in which a revolving cylinder,
covered with a black-lead paper, is set going, with a
pencil attached to some part of the patient's body,
according to the nature of the observation—attached
to a lever, and the lever in turn attached to the
body, so that any motion in that part of the patient's
body is reproduced by the pencil pressing against
the cylinder; as the cylinder revolves the pencil
would draw a straight line if there were no motion,
but any motion will produce a curve.

Now ,suppose you had such a machine attached
to your heart, you would get then a series of curves
traced on this black-lead paper showing the beating
of the heart, and the slightest irregularity in the
beating would at once be marked in a very magnified form in the curves traced by the pencil on
this cylinder. So again with any movement of the

lungs.   There is a definite movement of the lungs
and the curve would be recognised by any doctor.
So again, if you are dealing with muscular contractions.   If you stretch out your arm straight,
and you have a weight in the hand, there is action
taking place in the muscle—vibrations—and that
increases tremendously in activity as the arm is held
out longer and longer, the effort increasing with the
time of the extension of the muscle.

Now, all these precautions are taken in order to
eliminate every possibility of fraud or cheating, so
as to get an absolutely accurate physical record of
the state of the patient's body; and they have thus
shown that when a person is in a hypnotic trance
the beating of the heart is entirely changed, and
finally reaches a point so slight that although the
movement is still shown on the revolving cylinder,
no instrument less delicate would show it was beating at all.   The same with the lungs; the movement
of the lungs is so slight that no breath can be found
coming from the lips.   So also in regard to muscles.
There is a distinct trace which enables them to say
whether or not the man, with the outstretched arm
heavily weighted, is or is not in a hypnotic state.

Now, what is the condition of the brain when the
body is like that?   In the first place the blood supply
is checked.   The blood moves very sluggishly through
the vessels of the brain and in the tiny vessels, the

capillary vessels, its movement is stopped. Not only is the supply of blood in this way entirely changed in its motion, but the blood is very bad of its kind, for as it is not properly aired in travelling through the lungs, it is very much overcharged with all the products of decomposition, and you have quantities of carbonic acid. The result of that is very well known. It brings about a state of coma, a state in which no thought is possible, so far as the brain is concerned. So that we get a person who cannot think with the brain. The brain is stopped. It is placed in a state in which any one, twenty-five years ago, would have said thought was impossible. You have brought about a physical condition in which thought must vanish; and so it does, so far as that physical body is concerned. The creature lies there as though he were dead; but you are able to reach him without altering these physical conditions; you are able to obtain from him mental results, and when a person is in that state you can show that his mental faculties are immensely stimulated, that his memory has quite changed its character; that he can tell you incidents of his childhood which in his normal state he had entirely forgotten; that he will sometimes speak a language which he heard as a tiny child and has since entirely forgotten, so that if it is spoken in his presence he is not able to understand it. You will find that the memory is so in-tensified in its immediate action, leaving the past out of sight, that if you take up a Greek book and the man is ignorant of Greek, and you read over a page from that book, he will repeat it word for word without a blunder. Wake him up and he cannot say it, cannot pronounce a single syllable. Throw him back into the hypnotic state, and he will repeat it over again and again. Not only have you thus a very different kind of memory, but you also can obtain a far higher grade of intelligence. A person who is stupid in his waking consciousness is often clever when he is under hypnotic control; not that he reproduces the thought of the hypnotiser, as indeed he will do if he is made to, but he will dwell on things when the hypnotiser is thinking on other lines, and will argue with him. Cases are on record where a man normally stupid has shown acuteness in his argument when he is in a state in which the brain cannot work. And so over and over again you get placed on record these observations of abnormal knowledge, manifested when the brain is rendered incapable of sane and healthy thought.

The next thing that you remark in dealing with such a person is that you can entirely deceive the senses, and make them give reports which are entirely erroneous; that you can make him see what is not visible, and you can equally easily make him not see what is visible; that, for instance you could make yourself invisible, and if you like you can leave yourself tangible but invisible, so that he may walk right up against you as though you were not there and start, when on coming against you, he finds an obstacle that he cannot see. So you can alter the sense of hearing; you can make him hear or not hear, as you please. So you can, if you like, destroy the sense of touch so that he shall not feel, or you can do the opposite and you can make him feel a solid body by simply stating that it lies between his hands. You can make him smell a sweet odour when you present to him some repulsive article. You can play with the senses as you can stimulate the mind. You can prove still more than this by taking an ordinary person and thus hypnotising him.

I now pass from the Paris hospitals to statements made by doctors in care of the insane asylums. If you take an ordinary lunatic and throw him into the hypnotic state, you can obtain from him in some cases intelligence and reasoning power. The moment he is out of that condition he is again a lunatic, but under hypnotism he becomes an intelligent thinker.

Now, these things are done over and over again. Suppose you prove that instead of thought varying with the state of the brain it varies against it; that when the brain is in a state of coma, thought is exceptionally active; that when the brain is paralysed, memory is exceptionally acute and brings back events that are long forgotten; what is the inevitable inference? That although thought may continually be expressed through the brain, it is also possible to express it without the brain; that although it is true that many events remain in the normal memory and others are forgotten, those forgotten events are not really forgotten; they remain in consciousness, although out of sight; they can be brought up by consciousness, although normally they have vanished. So that you are led inevitably by these observations that can be repeated indefinitely, to realise that human consciousness is something more than is expressed through the physical brain.

I am not going to press the argument one bit beyond that, for the moment, but you do prove to demonstration that there is more consciousness in a man than comes out in his waking moments when the brain is in its normal state of activity; that he has a consciousness wider than the waking; that under abnormal conditions this consciousness emerges; that it contains the record of events that the waking consciousness has forgotten; that it is able to exercise powers keener and subtler than the powers of the waking consciousness. So that you finally come to the conclusion that whatever human consciousness may be—and on that at present we will not dog-

matise—that whatever human consciousness may be,
it is something more than that which we know in
our healthy waking moments, and that there is more
of us than is expressed through the brain, that we
are able to possess more in consciousness than our
brain allows us to express; and so we arrive at the
rather startling conclusion that the brain is a limitation placed on our consciousness; a partial instrument, instead of the producer, of thought.

That is, we have entirely reversed the materialistic
position. Instead of the brain producing thought
thought expresses itself partially through the brain.
As much of it as can get through comes through, and
the rest remains for the time unexpressed but not
non-existent. This is so much recognised now that
all these French schools will divide consciousness,
and tell you about the waking consciousness and the
dream consciousness, that which is called the sublim-
inal consciousness; there are all sorts of wonderful
terms, that I sometimes think do more to cover ignorance than to express knowledge, and we constantly find the most wonderfully complicated expressions which are intended to convey the idea that
I have put into rather rough phrase, that there is
more of us in consciousness than comes through the
brain.

Now, all these discoveries have very much in-
tensified scientific investigation along the lines of this

consciousness which does not work in the physical brain; and you have men like James Sully, men like Sidgwick, that are leading the English writers on psychology, giving a very large part of their time to the state of the consciousness which is outside the waking state. Why, some years ago, if people had studied dreams, they would have been thought as foolish as Theosophists are thought now; but to-day the study of dreams is highly scientific. You need not be the least afraid of losing your character as sane and rational people by the study of dreams. On the contrary, you will only be advanced people, going along the lines of the most advanced science, rather, in fact, beyond your neighbours than below them in intelligence; and this has been the result of finding out how much is to be learned by studies of the dream state; and that is our next step.

Now, there have been certain very interesting physiological measurements made, and if science is good at anything it is good at measuring. It is extra-ordinary the way modern science measures; the accuracy, the delicacy of it, the way in which by its balances it will weigh, I am afraid to say, how tiny a fraction of a grain; and there is nothing in which science has made more remarkable advance than in the exquisite delicacy of its instruments whereby it measures what would seem immeasurably minute results. And another thing that is admirable is the wonderful patience of these scientific investigators. Clifford once spoke of the sublime patience of the investigator; and the term is not misapplied. Their patience really is sublime. They will do the same minute experiment over a hundred, or two or three hundred, times in order to be sure that they are right; and I hold that to be a most admirable quality, both mentally and morally; morally, because it implies that love of the truth which will take unending pains before it will make an assertion or accept the record of a fact; and I say this all the more strongly because it is sometimes thought that Theosophy is against science. That is not so. We give the fullest admiration and homage to the patience and the care, the reverence for truth, shown by the modern scientific men. All we object to is when they make inferences too hastily, and then assert their inferences as definitely as they assert their facts. Then we get rather into quarrels sometimes with them, because we cannot take all the inferences they make, knowing as we do that the inferences are based on incomplete knowledge of the facts.

Now, one of the things that science has been measuring is the rate of the nervous wave in the physical organisation—how long it takes for a wave to pass along nervous matter, to be transmitted from cell to cell—a fairly difficult thing to observe, I mean with the accuracy with which it has been done; but some of our German friends, especially, who are nothing if they are not accurate, have gone very carefully into these measurements. They have found out the fraction of a second which it takes for a wave or vibration in nervous matter to occur, so that they are able to tell us exactly just how long it takes for such a wave of nervous motion to travel, and that means how many such waves can occur in any given track of nerve within a second of time. They can tell how many such vibrations can be received in a second. Let us suppose for the moment—for the number does not matter for our purpose—let us suppose that they found that nervous matter could receive a hundred vibrations per second. You know that the nervous matter of the eye, for instance, if it receives vibrations within less than one-tenth of a second, yields a continuous impression. If your impressions separated from others by more than one-tenth of a second, you see that impression by itself. Now apply that to the states of consciousness of the later investigations, and you find that a certain number of impressions can be made on the nerve, representing states of consciousness, or succession of thoughts. Let us suppose that a hundred of these can take place in one second. Now go to sleep and dream, and within one second of physical time you may have thoughts experienced by the intelligence at the comparative rate of four or five thousand or more in the second. You may live in the dream consciousness through a year, and every event may be there; you may go through them one after another; day after day, and night after night, you may experience successive events, you may live through troubles and joys; all these intellectual results may be experienced, and when you are awakened one second of physical time only has passed, and yet you have gone through states of consciousness that the nervous system would demand a year to accomplish. Nevertheless, you have thought; those states of consciousness have existed; you are able to recall them, and they have gone at this immense rate; your intelligence has been working at a hundred times the normal rate. What does this mean? It means that it has been working in a finer kind of matter. The finer the matter, the more rapid the vibrations; the finer the matter, the more vibrations can you get in that second. If you are dealing with ordinary nervous matter it moves comparatively slowly. If you are dealing with ether it moves at a tremendous rate; and if you are dealing with matter finer than ether, then inferentially the rate would be increased proportionately to the fineness of the matter in which the vibrations were set up.

If, then, you are able to think at a rate beyond your power of thinking in the brain, it means that your intelligence is functioning in something finer than the brain. I do not want to press it one bit further than it goes, but it does prove by demonstration that your intelligence is working in a medium finer than nervous matter. Whatever that medium is, it is very different from the nervous matter of the brain. It may be superethereal, as a matter of fact it is, but we are content to take up the position, that, whatever it is, it vibrates hundreds of times faster than any nervous matter can vibrate, and therefore the intelligence has some form of expression which is not an expression by the brain. This is the point to which you are led by an argument in which no flaw can be picked. It is the first time that science has given an argument, clear and definite and impregnable, which proves beyond possibility of challenge that intelligence in man does work at a rate which the brain is unable to satisfy, and therefore whatever intelligence is and does, the medium in which it is able to function is something other than brain.

Well, so far we have gone on ground that no materialist can deny. Our next step is to show that this intelligence which is not dependent on the brain, which is able to work without it, which works better without it than it does with it, more swiftly without it than it does with it, more keenly and acutely without it than it does with it—to show that

this intelligence survives death. And see how carefully we are going step by step. We are not hur-
rying in any way; we are not rushing over it; we
are only taking the next very quiet little step. We
have intelligence working without the brain while
the brain may be still, as you may say, in touch
with that intelligence; and now we are going to
kill our physical brain altogether, and see whether
the intelligence that functioned in it during physical life can be found functioning without it after
physical death. And here, of course, people who
believe in immortality have put themselves at a
great disadvantage with the logical materialist, by
making the life of the soul to begin at birth; because
it is obvious that if the soul cannot manifest at birth
without a body, then it seems as though it were
likely that it could not get on without a body, and
so death would very much paralyse its action. That
is due to a lack of philosophy which has been allowed to weaken much of our religious thought; and
the giving up of the reasonable philosophy of reincarnation, or pre-existence of the soul, has struck
the most deadly blow at all belief in the soul's immortality. Making it dependent on the body for its
manifestation, we imply its dependence on the body
for its further persistence. However, leaving that
point out, because it need not necessarily come into
our argument, we shall get the next definite proof

from the experiments of our spiritualistic brethren, or of such men as Professor Crookes, who, although he has always refused to definitely identify himself with the spiritualistic body, has yet convinced himself by his own careful experiments of the truth of many of their assertions. He is a very cautious man, and he does not use the word "spirit"; but he does show that intelligent entities, after they have been living in a physical body, do again function out of that body. Of course it is not necessary that the body should have perished by death, but in most of these cases, as a matter of fact, it has. If any of you will take the trouble to turn to Professor Crookes' investigations, in which he had the medium and what is called a materialisation—materialised soul, it is called, but that is a very silly expression —a materialised form present under his eyes at the same time, and read them carefully, you will be obliged to admit that there is evidence there worthy of further consideration. Of course if you have not read anything of the kind nor looked into it yourself, you will probably deny the possibility off-hand, because it is one of the characteristics of people that the less they know about a thing the more emphatically do they deny it. It is a great advantage to know nothing when you want to be what an English school-boy would call "cock-sure." I don't know whether you have the phrase over here, but it is an

ordinary bit of school-boy's slang, and it always
goes hand in hand with ignorance; but I never find
it in the scientific man. He is always cautious. He
says: "Well, I don't believe it; I don't think your
evidence is enough." He won't deny it; whereas the
ignorant person will deny with a vigor proportioned
to the depth of his ignorance. Now I am supposing
that somebody is willing to read; does not think he
knows everything in nature; does not believe that
everything within the universe is within the limits
of his knowledge. If a person has reached that not
very advanced position, he may condescend to look
into the evidence afforded by a man like Crookes.
He has, for investigating materialisations, invented
a convenient little lamp which lights as soon as it is
opened. The reason why he used that particular
kind of light was that it is very difficult to produce
a materialisation under the light-waves coming either
from gas or electric light. It is far easier to produce it in the dark. Now, of course, many people
begin to laugh the moment that is said; they say:
"Oh, yes, because it is fraudulent." That is not
so; an electrician cannot produce an electric spark
from his machine in a very damp atmosphere; and
if you said: "Oh, that is only because you want to
commit fraud," he would laugh at you. So it is
true that there are certain combinations of matter
which do not hold together under the vibrations of

ether set up by certain kinds of light. That is all the reason. It is merely that certain wave motions break up these aggregations of ethereal matter.

Now Crookes, being a chemist and an electrician, was too much instructed to take it for granted that the only reason why darkness was demanded was fraud. He thought there might be some other reason, and he invented a particular kind of lamp— some preparation of phosphorus it was—that the materialisation might take place in the dark, and that then by just opening the door of his lamp, the air would touch the preparation of phosphorus, and it would burn up and give light, so that all in the room would be clearly visible. He did this, and under these conditions he was able to see the medium lying on the sofa and touch the medium with one hand, the medium being dressed in black, while in front of him within his reach, and he allowed to touch it, there stood the materialised form in white; so that he had the two under his eyes at the same time; no curtains or dark cupboards or anything else, but the two there in full sight at the same time, and he was allowed to handle both of them together.

Now, that is evidence good enough for any reasonable person, if you can trust the accuracy and the honesty of the investigator; and I venture to say William Crookes' name is beyond all challenge for honesty, and beyond all challenge for accuracy of observation amongst scientific people, who know the kind of experiments that he has made.

Well, in addition to a number of experiments like that, he weighed some of these forms, and he made other machines which enabled him to test the force that could be exercised without any visible force being used, and so on; so that he was able to show definitely an intelligent entity able to recall the events of the past life, holding. long conversations with him after death had been passed through.

And that experience—not always with such care, to make it scientifically certain—has been repeated over and over again by thousands of spiritualists. It is foolish to deny these facts. They are on record, and if you choose may be re-verified if you are doubtful. Fraudulent occurrences have also taken place, but to deny all materialisations because of these is as though you were to deny that there is any such thing as good money, because coiners circulate false coin. Such events do occur, and anyone who goes into it knows that they occur; and I say that although I do not approve of that line of investigation, although I think it dangerous and mischievous, none the less, if a person be a materialist and has been led up to the point that we reach by the study of hypnotism and by the study of dreams, he may very well then clinch, as it were, his growing convictions by getting, or much better, by himself trying, some experiments along these lines. He need not go to a medium, as three or four people of the same family, sitting together, will very easily be able to convince themselves that intelligence does exist and function on the other side of death. That very simple fact can be proved over and over again, and it is not necessary to go to any professional medium; any three or four of you, who know each other as honourable men and women, may, if you choose, prove it for yourselves. I do not advise you to do this unless you are materialists. If you are, it is worth the risk for the certainty. If you are not, if already you believe in the existence of the soul, then you won't gain very much as to the nature of its existence in that way; and it is foolish to run into danger where there is no equivalent gain. But none the less we are led up, step after step, to the existence of intelligent entities whom we knew in the body and may know out of the body.

Another line of investigation here, unaccompanied by danger, is based on the fact that the soul of a person connected with a living body can pass out of that body by training, and assert itself independently of the body, both as regards itself, and, if it choose, as regards others.

Now, I am going to step outside the line which science would recognise or which can be verified easily by anyone. I am going now into the more

difficult experiments in regard to the existence of
the soul. These that I have dealt with hitherto,
anybody can repeat. They are the *a b c* of the
study. If you are materialists, begin with these,
and when you have gone through them you will
have convinced yourself that a living intelligence
can function without the assistance of. the brain,
in or out of the physical body. You will have gone
so far, and when you have reached that, you may be
willing to take the trouble necessary for the more
difficult experiments that follow, those which alone
prove the existence of the soul, though the others
prove the existence of intelligence outside the physical organism.

I am now going further. I mean by the soul a
living, self-conscious intelligence, showing forth
mental attributes at will, and able to show forth attributes higher than mental as it grows, develops
and asserts itself on higher planes than the physical
and the astral. As I say, the experiments now are
very difficult and training is wanted. The beginning of training along this line of work, which leads
us really into what is called the practice of Yoga, is
first to use your mind to control your body and your
senses, so as to convince yourself that the mind is
something higher than the body, more powerful than
the senses. Set yourself to work to check some expression of the senses to which you have habitually

yielded; cease taking some article of food that is very attractive; drop some form of drink that is very pleasurable and stimulating; leave off some form of physical pleasure to which you are particularly addicted. I do not mean give it up altogether, but give it up for a time, to show that there is something in you, to prove to yourself beyond possibility of dispute, that there is something in you that can control all that part of your nature which you call the senses or the bodily expression. Make yourself do a thing against the desire of the senses, and choose a time when the sense is rampant, when it is longing for that particular gratification, eager to have it, when the thing is right in front of you, and you are just putting out your hand to grasp it. Stop and say: "I am stronger than you; you shall not gratify that desire." The only use of the experiment is that it convinces you, as nothing else does, that you are not your senses, and not your body; that you are something higher—let us say for the moment, the mind, and that you can control this body and these senses that very often run away with you. I do not mean that you can always control them; you cannot until you practise; there will be . times when these senses, like unbroken horses, will, as it were, take the bit in their teeth and run away with the mind and everything else, and you plunge right after them; they carry you off, but you know even then that they are carrying you off, and you feel that they are stronger than you, and are having their way. In a sort of upside-down fashion, even then you will distinguish between yourself and the wild, headlong influences and impulses that hold you captive for the time.

Now, that is a very elementary experiment, but you had better do it so as to be sure there is something in you stronger than the senses. "Oh," you say, "yes, that is the mind. Of course I know my thoughts are above the senses; of course I know that my mind can control my body." All right, keep on doing it, and practise until the body is no obstacle at all; until you can starve all day long and be perfectly good-tempered, even to the last moment; until you can be very tired and exhausted by physical labor and be as bright and even-tempered and sweet-natured to a troublesome child as if you were as fresh as possible. That is what is meant by controlling the body. Keep on practising until you can do it. It is not much. Keep on doing it until you realise that your body is only your servant, or slave, acting or not acting as you like, and feel the sense of shame when the body is able to make you do what the mind condemns; feel that to do that is to be less than man, less than really human. Dogs snap when they are hungry or angry; human beings ought to be able to be self-controlled; and it is not much to ask that the man shall have control, which only means, after all, that his mind is master of his body.

So far, then, we shall agree. Let us suppose that you are now ready to take the next step. That mind of yours is a troublesome thing after all. It is able to control the body; it is able to control the senses. Is it able to control itself? You find it runs all over the place. You take up a very difficult book and you want to master that book. A good deal depends on your mastering it. Perhaps you are going to pass an examination. Unless you can master that book in the night-time you will fail and that will throw you back in your career; and you sit down and work at it; your mind wanders; when you want to concentrate on some mathematical problem, you are thinking, you find, of something quite different; your mind goes off and you have to bring it back; and this happens over and over again, and you put your book down and say: "Oh, I am not in the humour; I cannot do it." What sort of a mind is that? It won't work when it is wanted, and it can't do what is its special business, because it is not in the humour. And then you begin to say: "Why shouldn't I control the mind?" And in that very phrase you are asserting something that is higher than the mind—I. " I mean that this mind shall do what I want it to do, and be fixed on that book."

You concentrate your attention; you gather up something which is strong in you, and you fix the mind on that subject and you work at it. What is it that has done it? It can't be the mind, which has been running all over the place, that has done it. It is something that is there which is able to master the mind, and train it to the point where it is wanted to work. Then you feel: "That is the thing I am going to look for now. I have found that the mind is above the senses—I know that; but here is something which is above the mind, and I must go in search of that. Perhaps that is the soul. This force that I feel, which masters my vagrant mind, this strength that I find within myself, which groups my wandering thoughts and compels their obedience, what is that? That seems to be myself. I am controlling my mind." When that point is reached, and when the habit has been made of the mind being fixed on a thing to order, there will have grown up a very definite consciousness of a something which is behind that mind and masters it, as the mind did the senses, and then the student may think it worth while to take steps to find out what that something is ,and then generally he will have to ask somebody who has gone a little further in this than he has: "What is the next step that I ought to take? I find something here that is higher than, more than, the mind. How am I to find out what it is? And in some book that he reads, or by some one whom he meets who can explain it to him, he learns that there exist certain practices, definite practices—what is called meditation— and that by following out those he can develop that consciousness which is higher than the mind.

When a person has reached this point, if no other person comes in his way, you may be sure that he will find a book; he will take up a book in the public library and read it; or some friend will say: "Have you seen that book?" and will introduce the book to him. Somehow or other the book will come in his way. Why? Because there are always more advanced souls watching to see when any evolving soul reaches the point where it can take help, where it is ready for further help; and if there is not available someone in the physical body who can give the help that that soul wants, then it will be directed to the finding of the book where the practical teaching will be given. It is the action of the helpers of men, who come with a helping hand to that seeking soul and place within its reach the knowledge that is the next step in its experiments, and rules for meditation will be found, studied and practised and when those rules are studied and practised what happens is this: That with each day's meditation, the consciousness beyond the mind grows stronger, and stronger, more and more able

to assert itself, more and more, as it were, revealing
itself, until presently the whole centre of consciousness will be shifted upwards, and the man will
realise that he is not at all his mind, but a great
deal more than the mind, and he will then begin
to sense things that the mind cannot sense, become
conscious of thoughts that the mind is unable to
appreciate; and now and then there will come down
a great rush, as it were, of thoughts that dominate
the mind and that mind is unable to explain, although it realises them as true when once they are
presented to it. And then arises the question: ''I
did not argue myself up to this; I did not reach it
by logic; I did not reach it by argument; I did not
reach it by thinking. It came to me suddenly.
Whence did it come?'' And the consciousness arises
slowly: ''It came from myself; that higher part of
myself which is beyond the mind, and which in the
quiet of the mind is able to assert itself.'' For as
has often been said, just as a lake unruffled by the
wind will reflect sun, or mountain, or flowers, but
ruffled gives only broken images; so when the mind
is quiet the higher thought is reflected in the lake
of the mind, but as long as the winds of thought
blow over it, it is ruffled, and only broken images
are seen.

In the quiet of the mind, then, the higher thought
asserts itself.

Then comes another stage, a higher stage. The student tries more and more to identify himself with the higher thought; gropes after it, as it were; tries to feel it as himself; concentrates his efforts and keeps the mind absolutely still; and at some moment of that experience, without warning, without effort, without anything in which the lower mind takes part, suddenly the consciousness will be outside the body, and the man will know himself as the living consciousness looking at the body that he has left. Over and over again in different Scriptures this statement is found. You may read, for instance, in one of the Hindu Scriptures, that a man should be able to separate the soul from the body as you may separate grass from the sheath that enfolds it. Or, in another phrase, that when the man has dominated the mind, he arises out of the body in a brilliant body of light—a statement literally true. The body in which the soul arises is luminous, radiant, glorious exceedingly—a body of light. No words could better explain this appearance, no phrase more·graphically describe the man rising out of the physical body in the astral or in some higher body.

I quote that ancient Scripture in order that you may not for a moment imagine this is simply a modern investigation. All those who know the soul have passed through that experience. It is the final proof that the man is a living soul; not argument, not reasoning, not interference, not authority, not faith, not hearsay, but—knowledge. I am this living consciousness, and that body I have left is only a garment that I wore. It is not I; it is not myself. That is not I, I am here; that I have thrown off; I have escaped from it; I am free from it. And that experience mentioned in those ancient Scriptures is mentioned in other Scriptures, too; it is the invariable experience of the prophet, and the teacher, and the seer, for none can truly teach the things of the soul except by his own knowledge. So long as he is only repeating what intellectually he has learned, he may do a most useful work, but he has not that stamp of first-hand knowledge which carries conviction with it to those whom he teaches. Second-hand knowledge is always liable to be challenged. Questions may be asked which it is almost impossible to answer, if you are only repeating what you have learned intellectually. A necessary stage; I am not speaking against it. All go through it who reach the other. But if the world is still to have witnesses of the immortality of the soul; if the world of the nineteenth century is to have what the world has had in all other ages, the first-hand testimony of living souls that they know that they exist; then men in the nineteenth century must go through the same training that they have gone through in other times, for only thus is first-hand knowledge attainable, and the question of the existence of the soul is put for evermore beyond possibility of doubt or of challenge.

The first time there may be a sense of bewilderment, or confusion, or wondering what this strange thing is that has happened; but as it is repeated day after day, week after week, month after month, year after year, that consciousness outside the body becomes real, nay, far more real than that within the body; for, coming back into the body time after time, the soul experiences that entering the body is like going into a prison-house; that it is like leaving the open air and going into a cellar or a vault; that the sight is dimmed; that the hearing has grown almost deaf; that all the powers of the soul are limited and deadened, and that this body is indeed as S. Paul, the great Initiate, called it, the body of death, not the body of life.

We call this life; it is not life at all. We call it life; it is simply the limited, imprisoned, dulled, dwarfed existence, which the soul endures for a short time of its experience in order to gain certain physical knowledge which otherwise it would be unable to acquire for lack of suitable instruments. But as you become men of meditation, that higher life becomes a sort of dream, recognised as an illusion, as duties that have to be discharged, obligations that have to be paid, where much has to be done; but the world is a world of prison, of death, not the world of freedom, of life; and then we realise that we, ourselves, are that living, active, powerful, perceiving intelligence to whom the worlds lie open, for whom heaven is the native land, the natural and rightful dwelling-place.

These are the lines along which we pass to the final proof of the existence of the soul. See how gradual the stages have been; how we began on the physical plane with physical experiments; how we passed on then a little into the region of dreams, and action outside the body; how then we took up the question that we recognise by use the difference between the body, and the senses, and the mind; and then how we found the assertion of something beyond that mind more real and more powerful than itself; and then how, encouraged by those lower experiments, we penetrated into the higher, and paid the price which is necessary for that first-hand knowledge of the soul.

Truly, it is worth while. I do not pretend that it can be gained without paying the price. I do not pretend that you can enjoy vehemently the life of the body, and the senses and the mind, and at the same time carry on this evolution of the higher life; but this I tell you, that all that you lose is merely the pleasure which you have outgrown, and

which, therefore, no longer attracts you. You lose
that in the way that you lose your toys when you
\ grow out of childhood; you do not want them. It
is not that any one takes them away from you or
breaks them; you do not want them any longer;
you have found a higher enjoyment, toys of a finer
kind. But the mind is also a toy, though finer than
the toy of the senses; that also is recognised as a
toy in the higher regions of the life. Gradually
then, you give up those pleasures; they have lost
their savor; but you perform your duties better
than you have performed them before. Don't fall
into the mistake that some people do when they
begin meditating, of going about the world in their
waking life in a fog, in a dream, abstracted, so that
everybody says: "Why, that person is losing his
mind!" That is not the way to meditate. Meditation makes men more effective, not less keen, not
blinder; more alert, not less alert, less observant.
The stage wherein people are dreaming is a very
early stage of the training of the mind, when they
are still so weak that they cannot manage the mind
at all; and I have noticed over and over again, if
I take for a moment a personal illustration, that I,
who have done a good deal in this way of meditation, who have trained myself carefully along the
road that I have been pointing out to you, I often
notice when I am with people who have never

dreamed of this at all, and who call themselves quick, observant people of the world, that I see things that they miss, observe things that pass them unobserved, notice all kinds of tiny things in the streets, in the railway cars, in people, which pass them by without making the slightest impression. And I only mention that to show you that it is not necessary to lose the powers of the lower mind while you are busy evolving the higher. The fact is you have them much more at your command, and just because you do not wear them out by worry, and fuss, and anxiety, they are much more available when you want to use them; indeed, common sense is very marked, and reason, logic, intelligence, caution, prudence, all these qualities come out strongly and brilliantly in the true occultist. The man becomes greater and not less on the mental plane, because he works in a region beyond and above the intellect. He has gained in life. He is not robbed of the lower life; he has lost it, and in losing it he finds it. Resigning the lower, he finds the higher flowing into him fully, and the lower is more brilliant than it ever was before. He asks for nothing; everything comes to him. He seeks for nothing; all things flow to him unasked. He makes no demands; nature pours out on him her treasures. He is ever pouring forth all that he possesses. He is always full, though ever emptying himself.

Those are the paradoxes of the life of the soul; those the realities proven as true, when the existence of the soul is known, and if to-night I have not tried to win you by mere skill of tongue or picture, or what would be called appeals to emotion and feelings, it is because I wanted to win your reason step by step along this path; because I wanted to show you—without emotion, without appeals to intuition, without making, as I might make, appeal to that knowledge within every one of you—that you are immortal existences and that death is not your master. Instead of appealing to that, as I have the right to appeal to it, I have led you step by step along the path of the reason; I have shown you why you should take each new step when the others behind are taken. But let me, in concluding, say a word to those who do not need to take the lower steps of this toilsome path, who do not need to prove that the soul exists, who are filled with the consciousness that they are living souls, who, though they know it not at first-hand, by knowledge, yet have a deep, undying conviction that no logic can shake, no argument can alter, no scoff can vary, no jeer and no proof can change. Beaten in argument, confused by logic, bewildered by proof, they still say: "I feel, I know, I am a living soul." To those I would say: trouble not yourselves about the lower steps; trouble not yourselves with all the arguments I was using as proof over and over again re-iterated, intended to convince the materialist. Trust your intuition, and act on its truth. The inner voice never misleads. It is the Self whispering of its own existence and imperially commanding your belief. Yield your belief to the voice within. Take it for true, though you have not proved it as true, and act on that internal conviction as though it were true. Then begin the processes of meditation I hastily alluded to. Take, as you may take, the books where these are traced out for you one by one. Begin to practise them. Do not waste any more time in reasoning out other processes that you are not ready to understand. Trust the voice within you. Follow the guidance which has been marked out for those who have trodden that road and have proved it to be true. Then swiftly and easily you will gain the knowledge. Then, without long delay, you will know of your own knowledge that these things are true. If the soul speaks to you, don't wait for the confirmation of the intellect. Trust the divine voice; obey the divine impulse; follow out the road traced by sages, by prophets, by teachers, verified by disciples who, in the present day, have trodden it, and know it to lead to the rightful goal. Then you, too, shall know; then you, too, shall share; then your intuition shall be confirmed by knowledge, and you shall feel yourselves the

living, the immortal souls. That is my message to
you then, to those who need not the proof, who appeal to the intuition; and in giving you the message,
I speak not of myself; in giving you the message,
I bring you no new thing; I confirm to you in your
own day and time, what every prophet has asserted,
what every disciple has taught, what every divine
man has proclaimed. As a messenger of that Brotherhood, I do but repeat Their message.

There is the weight of the evidence, and not in
my poor reassertion of it. What is it that one soul
should have found to be true, that which all the great
souls have declared? If you would have authority,
take it on their word. Remember that what I speak
is indeed spoken with my lips, but with Their voice;
I bring to you the testimony of the ages; I bring to
you the message from an innumerable company. I,
but weak and poor in my own knowledge, limited
and circumscribed in my own experience, servant
of the great Brotherhood, holding it the proudest
privilege and delight to be able to serve and to give
my obedience, I speak Their word. I do not dare to
endorse it, as it were, though knowing it to be true.
I put it on Their testimony, unshakable, immovable,
back to the furthest antiquity, down to the present
day, an unbroken army of mighty witnesses, an innumerable company of prophets, of teachers, of
saints. Their messenger, I speak Their message.
You can prove its truth for yourselves, if you will.

Individuality

A Lecture delivered on Thursday, July 21st, 1898, to the Blavatsky Lodge, London.

One of the services which is rendered to thoughtful people by the Theosophical teachings is the shedding of light on many difficult subjects, on many of those problems that puzzle us both with regard to the individual and to society; and this particular problem of individuality is one which, especially at the present time, is giving much trouble to the more thoughtful amongst us. We see so plainly the evils which result from the over-assertion of the individual; we trace so clearly the social and other obstacles which arise in the path of progress in connection with the over-individualism, as we call it, of the day, as we are very apt to think in an unbalanced way, to be swung strongly to one side or the other by the things that strike us at the moment, we are a little inclined to look on this individualism, or individuality, whichever we may happen to call it, as a thing which is more or less evil in itself.

Hence continually, both from pulpit and from platform, we hear denunciations of individualism, and we find people continually told that they ought to learn to look at society as the life which is held in common, and that it is the great duty of each to subordinate his own interests to the common good.

Now that view of society is, as probably we shall all agree, a true one, when it is stated within right and due limitations. We ought to subordinate our separate interests to the common good, we ought to learn more and more to drop our thinking as to the separated self; we are gradually to transcend this heresy of separateness and to grow into a real unity. That is true. But, if we want to understand how we should grow, and if we desire to throw light on the steps that we have been treading in the past which make it possible that we should evolve into this unity, then it is necessary for us to understand something of the use of individuality, something of the purpose of the long ages of its evolution, something of the part that it has played in the growth of the human spirit. And it is to this that I specially desire to direct your thoughts this evening—a difficult subject, I know, but one which, looked at in the light of Theosophy, seems to me to be full of instruction and of illumination. Just in proportion as we see it in that light will the tangled skein begin to unravel itself, and we shall find that really instead of a tangle we have a clue which may guide us through the course of evolution and enable us to understand much of the "Why?" and the "Wherefore?" of the struggles that lie behind us, and of the struggles that lie around us at the present time. And it may be well to bear in mind that the use we can be to the community, and the value of the work that we can perform in the world, really depend upon our understanding the conditions amid which we are working. If, seeing the struggles of the moment, with all the suffering that accompanies them, with all the conditions that we find in our social state to-day, we permit our emotions entirely to run away with us, if we permit the distress which we see around us to over-balance our thought, then we become useless in proportion to our lack of intelligence, and the mere unregulated enthusiasm is apt to do as much harm on the one side as it is striving to do good upon the other. Above all things it is the duty of the theosophical student to learn balance, by understanding the conditions amid which he finds himself, to realise that the Hands that guide evolution are wise and strong as well as loving, and that when we are inclined to kick most hastily against the order of the world, the impatience has its root in ignorance and would be changed into a wise and persevering endeavour by knowledge.

We are familiar in our studies with the general

idea of the great stages of evolution, in one of
which we are at the present time. We have studied
something of what we call the great life-waves,
which, coming from the life of God, made evolution
possible in all its different varieties; we have learnt
something of the life which maintains all matter;
we have learnt something of the life which organises
all forms, and we have also tried to understand
something, in an elementary way, of the life which
we speak of as the human spirit, a life which, coming down from the Father of all Spirits, is found
in man in its triple manifestation. The lowest
aspect of this trinity is in course of evolution at the
present time.

This general outline will be familiar to every student amongst us, and it is of course the third of
these outpourings of the Divine Life with which
we are concerned when we come to study the problem of individuality. It attaches itself especially
to what we have learnt to call the causal body in
man; that is, a high and subtle vehicle of consciousness belonging to the intellectual plane, and enabling the intellectual side of consciousness to develop as an aspect of the trinity, Man. This causal
body, we have learnt from our great teacher, H. P.
Blavatsky, endures throughout the cycle of incar-
nations. That is one of its distinctive marks, and in
that way it differs from the other visible and in-

visible bodies which make up the vehicles of consciousness.

Let me just remind you very hastily of the names
of those lower transitory vehicles and of the point
at which each of them breaks up, giving back its
materials to that plane of the universe to which it
belongs; and let me also remind you that every one
of these vehicles belongs to the form-side of evolution, to the side which shows form, and which is
therefore but the vehicle of life. The evolving consciousness itself is the life-side of manifestation,
whereas the forms through which it expresses itself
make up what we continually call the matter or form-
side of that same manifestation. Now these forms—
all of which, in the broadest sense of the word, are
transitory even the causal body, relatively permanent as it is—these forms, beginning at the lowest, are: the physical body, which lasts the ordinary
life-period upon earth, which begins to disintegrate
at death, and which, both with regard to its dense
and its etheric parts, does not subsist for very long
after death. Its molecules resolve into their chemical
constituents, and are again worked up into other
physical organisms. But, as that body perishes, it
hands on that which it has gathered during its existence in the world to the invisible bodies with which
it was connected during life. Some of you who may
be familiar with the *Upanishads,* those great Scrip-

tures of the eastern world, may remember a very striking passage in which the withdrawal of life is described, and as the body is dying a description is given of how life, prâna, withdraws itself from the body, and how in withdrawing itself it gathers up that which has been experienced during the life and takes it with it. As this prâna retreats into the astral body and the astral world, it carries with it into the world the experiences gathered in the physical, and when the time comes for the astral body to break up, as it does at some period, generally a longer period, after death, it again hands on to the higher body that which can endure in the heavenly world, the results of its experiences and of its workings upon those experiences. The life-breath centres itself in the mental body in the heavenly world, having carried up with it these experiences, each set becoming latent at a certain point where they are no longer able to express themselves for lack of suitable form, but remaining latent, and able to come again into expression when a suitable form shall be evolved, when the time for reincarnation arrives. But this heavenly life also is transitory, it also passes away, and when the mental body, which endures during that life, in its turn breaks up, it does the final handing on of all the life's experiences then gathered up into itself, it passes them on into the relatively permanent body, the causal body, or body of causes. The name is given to it because in it everything is gathered up, and when the time comes for reincarnation everything is put out from it on the successive planes. Everything being gathered up into this causal body, it remains as the vehicle, the reincarnating ego, as we often call it. When the time for its reincarnation comes, it draws round itself the necessary vehicles on the lower planes, and so builds up once more the total constitution of the man. Inasmuch, then, as this is the only body of man that endures from life to life, we may regard one of its great functions as being that of the receptacle of all life experiences. Some of these are worked into its own nature, some of them serve to build up its own fabric; but it is only the higher of these experiences which are able to contribute to the building up and to the growth of that lofty and sublime body. High intellectual achievement, noble aspiration, endeavours which have their root in the inner nature of man—all these help to build it up, to make it stronger, to increase the ego itself, and so to make it an ever-expanding consciousness, able to function more and more fully and more potently on the different planes.

The lower experiences which are gathered up, and which cannot directly contribute to the building of this sublime body of the ego, are, after assimilation,

put forth, in the way at which I have hinted, in
the successive stages of reincarnation, forming in
their turn the vehicles of the new life, the mental
and the emotional bodies, and then in due course
influencing the building up of the physical body
which is to be the expression in the physical world
of the consciousness, so far as within the limits of
the physical body that consciousness is able to express itself.

Recognizing, then, the great function of the
causal body as the receptacle of life's experiences,
the next statement which I made, that only some
of these experiences, those of a lofty character, can
be built into its own nature, leads us to this next
truth regarding the evolution of the man, that on
the building in of these higher experiences his whole
evolution as a human being, as an individual, depends. The causal body represents the individual;
it separates him from other like individuals and
from all other objects in the universe. It is like a
case, or an egg, as it has sometimes been called,
within which all is stored, but the wall or shell of
which shuts out the consciousness from all other
forms of consciousness which live and move around
the man. So that this causal body may be said to
make the individuality. We may, in fact, call it
the individual, and this true individual is continually growing by all the higher and nobler thoughts.

This fact may explain to you a statement that has often been made—that the evolution of man in the earlier stages is exceedingly slow, but that it quickens rapidly as he advances. For inasmuch as in the more advanced soul there will be a far larger proportion of the higher intellectual activities, of the nobler aspirations, these contributions to the growth of the individual will be very much greater in the later than in the earlier stages of his evolution.

There is one other function that the ego, or causal body, discharges, and it is the function of protection. By this I mean that the outpoured life of God, which is the living human spirit, has gradually to establish itself as a self-conscious centre. That self-conscious centre will take long in building, and during its building and its evolution it may be thought of as surrounded by this protective shell or wall, which enables it to grow and to develop and to expand without being, if I may use the phrase, scattered in space; it serves as a containing vessel in which the life may develop all its powers; it protects that life while transmitting to it every contact from without which will evolve the responsive powers within. At the same time it serves as a protective envelope, enabling the consciousness gradually to form its own strong centre which, later on, as we shall see at the close of our study, will

be able to subsist for endless ages without the protection of this limiting wall, having lost in essence
nothing it has gained during its pilgrimage, but
being no longer limited in the sense of being separated from others by this dividing shell, which is
nevertheless necessary for all the processes of its
human growth and evolution.

Now there is one point of importance to remember in connection with the causal body and with
regard to its growth. I have spoken of its growth
by means of high aspirations, high intellectual
thoughts, and so on, and the question naturally
comes to the mind: "Is it possible for a man to
injure the causal body, say by a vicious life?" Just
as a man by his lower experiences is not contributing
directly to the growth of the causal body, but to
that reflection which we call the personality, of which
I will speak in a moment, so with regard to what we
may call the ordinary vices, they cannot be considered as injuring this lofty vehicle. In the lower
stages, when vice is ruling the man, and when his
passions are running headlong, the causal body is
comparatively undeveloped, and the rush and whirl
of passional activity are not able to affect to any
evil purpose this vehicle of the slowly evolving ego.
But as evolution proceeds, as the mental and intellectual consciousness develops, as the power of the
man grows in the mental world, then it is possible

that just as his noble thoughts and lofty aspirations
contribute so largely to its building, so when we
come to deal with the higher forms of evil, with intellectual pride, intellectual ambition, intellectual
selfishness—the subtlest and strongest of all the obstacles to the spiritual evolution—when we come to
deal with these, we find that they are able to affect
injuriously the causal body. For belonging by their
nature to the world in which this vehicle is evolving,
they are necessarily able to play upon it and ,to
affect it as injuriously as the corresponding lofty intellectual influences affect it for good. So that,
speaking broadly, we may say that the great mass
of human kind, passing through the lower stages of
evolution, cannot injure this vehicle as the more
highly evolved are able to do. They are passing
through stages in which the true individuality is
scarcely as yet being evolved, and consequently, however repellant much of their life may be, however
offensive and disgusting many of their vices may
seem, they are not in reality doing as much injury
to evolution as is done by the subtler and keener
vices of the more highly evolved man who, just because he is coming to his kingdom as an individual,
has powers which, if they are used for unselfish
service, will be lifting him towards the unity of the
spirit, but which, if they are prostituted to that selfishness which we ought to be outgrowing, will form

fetters the most difficult to break, fetters which will
possibly bind him prisoner for many an age to
come.

This very general glance at individuality will
give you the scope of our subject so far as its evolution is concerned. But now we must consider the
lower stages of the building, those steps which are
absolutely necessary before the higher can take place
at all, and which are connected with what I have
spoken of as the personality, which is the reflection
of the individuality, its image in the lower worlds.
Now it is of course this personality which is at first
evolved by man, and it is very necessary that we
should realize clearly what has often been said here:
that experience of every kind is necessary in order
that the personality may be built, and in order that
by its slow contributions that which shall become
later the individual may begin what we may almost
call the unconscious stages of its life. For there is
in every truth a period of what might be called the
gestation of the ego in the higher world, a time
when its consciousness is dim, but yet is beginning to
respond, when the thrills of its life are beginning to
answer to the impacts that strike it from without,
and when those impacts made through the senses
on the astral body and handed on through it and
through the inchoate mental body to the causal,
strike upon it, and though they cannot contribute

to its actual building, none the less do stir the life which is protected and guarded within it. All the earlier out-thrillings of that life will be in response to these violent impacts that come to it from outside; for never forget that all the life in you is Divine Life, the seed of God which is planted and is growing within you, and that every impact which strikes upon you from without is one of those blows of experience necessary to call out the corresponding answer from the life which is at first sleeping within. That life is awakened by these heavy blows of experience that come by way of the senses and the passions, and all these are absolutely necessary in order that it may be brought out of latency into activity. It is necessary, therefore, that man in these earlier stages should be passing through the various experiences that at our higher stage of evolution we rightly call "vicious." But remember that whether a thing is right or is wrong for any given individual depends upon the stage which that individual has reached in evolution. Whatever draws him downwards towards the life he ought to be outgrowing, that for him is vicious; whatever lifts him upwards towards the life to which he is climbing, that for him is right. It is inevitable, then, if we realize what evolution means, that according to the rung of the ladder upon which a man is standing will be the rightness or the wrongness of his activities in response to the impacts that come to him from the outer world; what is above him when he is standing at a very low stage will be below him when he is standing at a higher stage; and this continual change in the nature of morality, as it affects him, is a change which is necessary to understand and to appreciate if we are to take any intelligent view of the growth of the soul.

Let us now consider for a moment the evolution of the personality, and we shall see that it is absolutely necessary—in order that it may become vivid and strong and able to equip the lower mind with all the mental faculties which are necessary as the basis of the higher growth of man—that this evolving entity should pass through a period of strife, of labour, of struggle, of competition of every kind, otherwise the latent powers that **are** within could never be brought into activity. And what we call selfishness, and rightly deprecate at our present stage of evolution, at least in its grosser forms, is an absolute necessity for the evolution of the individual, since the individual cannot grow at all until the personality has reached a comparatively high stage of evolution. So that it is absolutely necessary, in order that the man may evolve, that he should grasp at all he can reach, that he should hold whatever he can grasp, and that he should fight for it against all who would take it from him. We shall see, therefore, as the necessary early stages of evolving humanity, a scene of combat, a strife, in which the man is fighting for his own hand, is fighting to hold his own place, is endeavouring to strengthen himself and his capacities in every possible way. And inasmuch as every power can only be evolved and made really potent by exercise, these conditions of struggle are necessary for the evolution of his powers, and if he did not pass through them he would simply remain for ever a mere undeveloped, unformed creature, a mere babe, as it were, in the womb, without the possibility of any higher development. In order to form the basis on which the stronger individuality is to grow up, he must develop all his mental capacities, and for their development it is absolutely necessary that he should pass through this life of combat; he must develop the power of distinguishing between one thing and another, and that he will do only by continual choices, which will be wrong over and over again for many and many a life; and in order that his choice may be effective, he must seize the thing he chooses and take it and keep it for his own, so that he may be able to appreciate the full results of that holding. How would he ever learn to distinguish between the different values, between the innumerable objects which surround him in the world; how would he be able in the study of his own emotions, in the study of his own passions,

to understand whether his choice contained good or
evil, harmony or disagreement, if he did not grasp
and hold until the full results were worked out in
his own life? Both sides must be taken, otherwise
neither side could ever be known, for only by the
knowledge of both can we learn to appreciate either,
and only as the pair of opposites is known can either
come out strongly as an object of consciousness. Selfishness, then, is a perfectly necessary stage in human
growth, a stage which is necessary in order to build
up first a firm and definite personality and later a
strong individuality, and to enable these to hold
their own against all opposing influences; and this
for the very purpose that the life within may develop, that the life within may be thoroughly
evolved, and that as the man advances he may become more and more able to stand on his basis firm
and unshaken, choosing with an ever-growing discrimination and with an ever-widening experience.
And tracing this still further, we shall find that this
development of the self-assertive individuality is the
special work of what we call our fifth race, just because at that stage of evolution the intellectual
growth is the special work to which the forces of
nature are turned. And inasmuch as the intellect is
the separative principle, working in the causal body
which holds itself apart from all others, and encloses
the life within it as it develops, it is this separate

self-assertive growth which characterizes the evolution of the fifth race, and which will be found in its very keenest point in the fifth sub-race to which we physically belong. Hence the tremendous competition in which these modern races are involved; hence the continual social strife in the midst of which this fifth sub-race is carrying on its development; hence the combat of one man against another, the grasping and the holding and the striving which meet us on every side. And yet amid all that whirlpool of contending forces, amid all that terrible battle of passions and of mental faculties, the eye of wisdom can discern the clear evolution of this necessary faculty, this necessary aspect of man—necessary for all its future growth and usefulness—the development of that self-conscious individual who will presently transcend the limits of individuality which have been the necessary conditions of his growth, and yet keep his centre unshaken even in all the intensity of the life of God.

Let us consider how the training of the race is proceeding as it is working on the individual as well as on the race. As this fifth race develops along its own lines, we notice that the individuals in it are being subjected to a double training, one which goes on in the society or the state of which they form a part, the other which goes on in the family of which they also form a part. And these two trainings are to a large extent contrary in their tendency. The life of society, as it exists to-day, strengthens, has strengthened still more in the past, and will continue for some time to strengthen, this sense of the individual, making him fight for his own place and his own position. I need not remind you of the terrible competition which is going on in our modern life, and of the effect that it is necessarily having on the evolution of all men and women amongst us; but if you look closely you will notice that a change is gradually coming over what we may call the social thought of our day. More and more there is asserting itself in society what we sometimes speak of as the social conscience; more and more we are beginning to recognise the duty which each one owes to the whole; more and more we see gleams of the recognition that man is one as well as many, and that his higher evolution will consist in the conscious realization of that unity and in the subordination of the clashing individualities into one harmonious chord of life. We find this view of human evolution making way amongst us, not yet very largely affecting the common life, but affecting the common thought, and that must necessarily precede any manifestation of that thought in the life.

Now unity is the note of the race that lies beyond our own, in which the spiritual nature is to be the evolving and finally the dominating principle. It finds its expression in brotherhood, in the using of strength for service instead of for combat, in the protection of the weaker instead of trampling them down, in the constant effort to realize a nobler and a higher life for all, in the pouring of the possessions of the individual into the common stock. The intellectual recognition of human brotherhood precedes its realization in the race that lies before us, and as the dawn of the next branch of our own fifth race, the sixth sub-race, slowly approaches, we shall see some glimpse of that recognition showing itself in our ordinary social life. And when we find appearing amongst us to-day, as we do find, efforts to diminish competition and to increase co-operation, efforts to help the weaker and the degraded and the ignorant, we see the dawning of that nobler ideal, we see the possibility of humanity evolving on to a higher plane. But in recognising it, we are able to trace a force which is at work to bring about that effect in society; and it is the force that lives in the family, in the training that individuals are there receiving, which I spoke of as being in its tendency antagonistic to the social training which they are receiving outside the home; for whereas outside they are still continually competing, in the family they are continually sharing; whereas in the outer society each man is fighting for himself, within his family he is constantly yielding that which he has gained for the helping of its weakest members. And more and more we see that in the family a common interest is recognized, that it is no longer a question of each member earning for himself and spending for himself and living for himself, but that the idea is there definitely recognized, and even taken for granted, that the older and the stronger and the cleverer are those who ought to bear the family burden, and share whatever advantages their higher capacities may bring them with those whose less developed powers render them less capable of making their own way in the world. So that in the life of the home and in the training of the family the individual is gradually being subjected to these unifying influences.

But at once the thought will arise in the minds of some: "Yes, but this is only after all what is sometimes called a wider selfishness; it is quite true that within the family circle you may find this unselfishness and this willingness on the part of the elder, say, to work for the younger and to deny themselves in order that the younger may have a greater share; but after all that is only an extension of the selfishness which fought for the individual to the selfishness which fights for the family. Supposing the man, his wife and his family make another unit, that unit asserts itself against all the other family units and competes with them, although within the limits of the family the struggle may have passed into the nobler side of self-sacrifice and common service." That of course is true. But there is no way of growth save by this slowly widening process; there is no way of rising save by treading the rungs of the ladder one by one; and although it is perfectly true that selfishness does play a very large part within this circle of the family, regarded as in opposition to all other families in the struggle for existence, none the less is it true that that wider selfishness is a step upwards, and that something is gained when the individual is not struggling merely for himself, but also for the little group of individuals linked to him by ties of kinship, of love and of duty.

And this brings me to the next principle of evolution that we must recognize if we would grow in reality, instead of wasting all our time in thinking how beautiful growth is and how much we should like to carry it on, and it is this: that we cannot do everything at once but can only rise step by step, that we cannot leap from the state of the sinner to the state of the saint by a single spring, and that we must learn to use even our vices as steps, and gradually to evolve first the lower virtues, and then to use those as stepping-stones to the higher, and the higher as stepping stones to the highest. To put that abstract statement into more concrete form, it

means this: that instead of struggling after some
object which gives us satisfaction in the lower part
of our nature, we gradually conquer that longing
by striving after the satisfaction of a higher stratum
in our nature. For instance, if we find that we take
great pleasure in the gratification of the lower senses,
we shall not try to fight tremendously against that
gratification when the opportunity presents itself,
but shall rather try to make it lose its attraction by
bringing forward a higher gratification, such as giving pleasure to one whom we love. Suppose, for
instance, that a man is addicted to the vice of gluttony, and realizes that if he gives way to that vice
his wife and family will go short of some of the
necessaries or the comforts of life; that man may be
fighting vigorously against his fellow-men, he may
even sometimes be unscrupulous in the method of
his fighting as he tries to gain advantages for himself and those who belong to him; but if within the
circle of his family he begins to check the vice of
gluttony, by giving up something even for the narrow and really selfish love for his wife, a love based
on his passion for her, on the satisfaction that he
gains by her company and by the help of her life in
the home, even then the man has made a step upwards. Certainly he is not yet particularly virtuous,
but inasmuch as he has given up something that
gave him a purely personal and selfish gratification

for the sake of giving more comfort to one whom he recognizes as having claims upon him, to whom he gives even a lower form of love, that man has made one step upwards in evolution; he has evolved a virtue, even though it be of a comparatively low kind, and he has killed a vice in that evolving. True, he will find personal gratification in the pleasure that he gives to wife or child; he will find satisfaction to his emotional nature in seeing the pleasure that he has given; but we ought not therefore to denounce the man as selfish and to discourage him by telling him that he is only showing another phase of selfishness, because for him it is a comparatively unselfish action, and so is building up a higher stage in his nature, even although presently he will outgrow that also and reach a nobler and a more unselfish love. And thus we find—looking at the two great lines of human evolution, the intellectual and the emotional—that progress along those two lines will be made by motives which attract first the personality and then the individuality, in each case because of something which they bring to that separated self. We may trace the growth and evolution of the man by the nature of the object that exercises this attractive power, and while it is still the separated self that is moved into activity by that which attracts it, none the less is evolution clearly marked if the nature of that attractive objcet is steadily rising in the scale of being. Consider, for instance, what is a very common motive amongst us—the desire to know. We desire to learn, to gain knowledge of various kinds, and this in order that we may become more highly trained, more highly evolved and developed. That motive to gain knowledge for oneself is an exceedingly powerful motive in evolution and an exceedingly useful one. By virtue of that motive men and women at the present time are dominating their animal nature, and learning to conquer the lower passions, are learning to live frugal, careful and abstemious lives. There is many a young man and young woman at the present time in this city and in our own society, who has to choose between a gratification for the body and some advantage that he may gain for the mind— to choose, say, between a costlier dinner and the buying of a book. Now it is perfectly true that in the buying of a book he may be moved by the selfish desire to possess, but it is a thousand times better for his evolution that he should be moved by the desire to gain the book and should spend his money on it, than that he should waste his money on the passing gratification of the physical body. And inasmuch as that desire for knowledge will teach him temperance and self-restraint, will keep him back from indulgence in vice, will teach him to live plainly in order that he may encourage and make

possible for himself high thinking, we ought to encourage him in that desire instead of saying to him
that he is prompted by a selfish motive and that he
ought to throw it aside and work for some abstract
thing that he does not in the least understand. For
although knowledge is being aimed at only to
strengthen his own individual growth, yet it is a
most valuable force in that upward growth, and he
will really kill out the lower by grasping after the
higher, even though it be entirely for the separated
self. Presently, as he gains more and more knowledge, that very knowledge will teach him that he
cannot evolve perfectly without helping others to
evolve side by side with himself, that he cannot go
on alone and leave his race utterly behind; and so
he will gradually learn to use his knowledge to
teach those who are more ignorant than himself,
and will thus take another step in his upward climbing. But let him keep the gaining of knowledge as
his motive so long as he needs it in order to spur
him into activity, sure that even as he gains more
knowledge he will widen out, his consciousness will
expand, and that then higher motives will begin to
attract and to exercise over him their inspiring force.
And these higher motives will come to him also as
he more and more develops in himself the emotional
side of love; for as the intelligence develops the man
will make for himself ideals; he will see noble lives

as he studies the past and the present, and looking
at these noble lives they also will exercise over him
an attractive force. He will wish to realize in himself something of the nobility that he sees, and he
will feel his nature drawn out towards those greater
men and greater women in love, in reverence, in
emulation. And as he begins to lead the life of
love, a love which pours out to those immediately
around him, with whom he is connected by all natural ties, as it flows out to those in his immediate
circle whom he recognises as more unselfish, more
compassionate, more pure, more developed than himself, this outflow of love and of reverence will raise
his nature, even though it be in many, nay, in all its
earlier stages, very largely selfish in its character.
He may be drawn to some friend who attracts him
by the nobility of his character; inevitably, as he
is drawn to that man and gives him love, he will
desire his company, will wish for his approbation,
will seek his affection, will look for return for the
love that he gives; and all these things will stimulate him into an attempt to be worthy of that love
which he desires to obtain. Shall we check that
which is working for growth by telling him that his
love is personal and selfish, by telling him that he is
after all only trying to gain for himself the affection that he desires from the object towards whom
his love is turned? Shall we tell him that it is only

after all another form of personality, of selfishness, of idolatry? If we do, and if we succeed in persuading him of the truth of what we say, we shall have deprived him of the greatest possible opportunity for his growth. Granted that much of selfishness mingles in that love, granted that much of personality clings to it, granted that one of his great objects in trying to be purer and wiser, more balanced, more noble, is in order that he may obtain the smile of approval from the one whom he recognises as his superior and, for the time being, as his ideal; yet surely that motive is bringing him the very evolution of which he stands in need. As he develops the higher purity, the greater, nobler thought, as he learns by his very admiration to bring out in himself the qualities that he admires in the one whom he loves and reverences, the bringing out of those qualities will purify the love, and all that is limited in it will gradually fall away as the expansion of the whole nature in the sunshine of that affection purifies and enobles it year after year. And that much decried hero-worship at which so many scoffs are thrown to day, which we so often hear spoken of as a sign of weakness and of folly, is in very reality not a sign of weakness but a sign of strength, for it shows the capacity to recognize that which is admirable when it is seen; it shows the power to reverence that which is great when it is met. There is nothing which more firmly holds the human soul in bonds, which more vulgarizes it and keeps it to a lower level, than the incapacity to recognize the great when we come into contact with it and to give greatness that love, that reverence and that homage which are really most potent means towards the growth and the evolution of the soul. We cannot, little developed as we are, recognize the abstract glory of Deity, the illimitable perfection out of which our life has sprung, but we can recognize the gleams of that beauty in noble and saintly human lives. Present it to us in individual and concrete form, and we are able then to recognize it and to feel its subtle and rare attraction; but if we cannot recognize it as it comes to us through the individuals within our sight, we are only deceiving ourselves when we dream that we recognize and worship it in the higher forms in which it exists in God. There is a true and noble saying of our great poet Browning, who, when speaking of the Hero-Souls of the world, of those who have served as Ideals and Models for mankind, writes:

> Through such Souls alone
> God, stooping, shows sufficient of His light
> For us i' the dark to rise by.

A profound truth nobly spoken. For all the beauty that is seen in any human soul is the divine beauty; all the love and the compassion and the purity that we recognize and love when we meet them in some flower of humanity, is God shining through that human form, which enshrines Him as the casket enshrines the jewel. Never be afraid to love or to reverence, never be afraid to give yourself wholly where you see that which is greater, grander than yourself. Let your love be imperfect for the time—it must be so while we are imperfect; let it be limited for the time—it must be so while we are limited. How should we, with our limitations, our follies, and our weaknesses, give a love that is flawless, perfect and divine?

Thus looking at growth, thus understanding how the individual develops, thus realizing that the highest individuals with whom we may come into touch are for us the divine images by which we shall grow into the divine likeness, amid all the puzzles and the tangles of the world, we may yet find a way in which our feet shall safely walk. And to what end? I spoke in the beginning of the transcending of the individual, of the purpose that the envelope of individuality served as the life within it grew into a strong, self-conscious centre. The day will come for each of us when the limits that enclose us will fall away; when the divine life within us will be able to hold itself as centre without need of the circumference to guard, to protect, and to enfold; when we, as living self-conscious centres, shall know ourselves in that life, and our consciousness shall expand to the consciousness of God, able to live in those ineffable vibrations which, encountered to-day, would but paralyze and make us unconscious. The day will come when, having utilized this individuality to the full, and having gathered up everything it has of lesson and of strength, we shall be able to stand without it in the divine light, stand as centre without that limiting circumference. Then will come the higher glory that shines yet beyond, when those living centres in divinity can come forth again when there is need for their aid, able in worlds and in universes to be the manifested expression of the divine love, the divine power and the divine perfection. When that happens we speak of the appearing as God made manifest in flesh; then truly the individual has vanished, then truly the limits have fallen away, but that living, self-conscious Being, He perishes never. In the glory of the divine flame that spark of light is seen, able to live, eternal, unshaken, able to come forth therefrom for service, able to share the consciousness of God and yet to come forth into the universe to express the divine Life, as Those only who have thus realized can express it. That will be the result of this growth of individuality, that the glorious ending, so far as we can see where ending there is none, of all these limitations that are encircling us to-day. And we realize that for such achieving all these stages of lower growth are absolutely necessary, every step in that growth becomes beautiful, and upon every stage in that evolution the light of Deity shines. And we know that, low as we are in our climbing now, the ladder that we are climbing has its ending in the divine light, and up that Jacob's ladder we too shall go from step to step, until we reach the stage where, as the Angels, we can descend for the helping of worlds as well as ascend to the throne of God.

Emotion, Intellect, and Spirituality.

A Lecture delivered on Thursday, July 7th, 1898, to the Blavatsky Lodge, London.

There is so much confusion of thought with regard to the meaning of the three stages of consciousness which I have described under the names Emotion, Intellect and Spirituality, that I think we shall not waste our hour this evening if we devote it to the consideration of these stages of consciousness, trying to define them accurately and to understand exactly what is meant by the name which is given each. And it is not only that by this study we shall, perhaps, somewhat clarify our ideas, but also we shall find that answers present themselves to certain rather curious problems that appear in human life from time to time, problems that are puzzling in their nature and that give rise to a good deal of bewildered questioning. We find people, for instance, asking why it is that we sometimes see an apparently fundamental change take place in a person within the limits of a single incarnation, and why someone who looks by no means hopeful during the

earlier stages of his life should perhaps evolve very
rapidly during the last half of his incarnation. Then,
again, another question that sometimes arises is:
Why is it that people who in many ways do not
seem to be qualified, show none the less certain signs
of spiritual growth? What is there in their nature
which enables them to acquire certain spiritual faculties, when, looking at them from the purely external standpoint, they would not seem to be sufficiently evolved to show forth these qualities? Why
is it, as I have often heard people say, that you can
sometimes obtain better and wiser advice from a
person in whom the higher intellect is not largely
developed, but who shows very strongly the qualities of compassion, benevolence and sympathy, than
from an intellect far more highly trained, than from
a well-developed mind?

Now if these stages of consciousness are not understood, we are apt to answer such questions in a
very mistaken fashion; and in a fashion, moreover,
that is not only mistaken in itself, but is also likely
to give rise to certain serious mistakes in conduct,
certain grave blunders in our attempts to forward
our own evolution. Thus we find people sometimes
mistaking abounding emotion for spirituality, sometimes confusing the mere surging up of feeling with
the strong potencies that come down from the spiritual world; and it is partly in order that we may

avoid those blunders, that I am going to ask you to follow me this evening in a somewhat careful analysis of these stages of consciousness, bringing them under the light of that Theosophical teaching which has illuminated for many of us so many problems in the past, and which illuminates so many new problems now.

If we look at the question from the ordinary standpoint of western psychology we find in our text-books the very familiar division of the mind into emotion, intellect and will. When we come to look a little more closely into this classification, we find that under the heading emotion sub-classes are made: first, "sensations," simple, primitive in their character, lying at the root of all further manifestation of consciousness, sensations which are the response of the organism to stimuli, to something that touches it from without. Then we have "feelings," which are said to arise from the grouping and co-ordination of these primitive sensations, complex in their nature—sometimes exceedingly complex —but none the less traced down to these simple sensations, which, grouped together according to their nature, gradually produce that which is recognized as feeling; so that under this heading, emotion, we have the two sub-classes of sensations and feelings.

Now if we consider for a moment the five planes of the universe on which, according to the Theosophical teachings, our human evolution is proceeding at the present time—the physical, the astral, the mental or mânasic, the buddhic and the nirvânic —if we consider for a moment those five planes, we shall see that they seem to arrange themselves in a very definite order. With regard to the nirvânic plane we need say practically nothing to-night, for although that be the higher region of the spiritual universe, it can scarcely come into our consideration at the present stage of evolution. The nirvânic and the buddhic planes together we class under the heading spiritual. All their forces would be spiritual forces, all consciousness working in them would be a consciousness spiritual in its nature, spiritual Beings would there have their habitat. If, then, omitting also for the moment the mental region, we look at the two lower planes—the astral and the physical—we find that these may be classed together as phenomenal. In these phenomenal worlds evolution takes place with regard to the astral body, the etheric double and the dense physical. These three bodies belong, of course, to the astral and the physical planes, which are capable of being classed together as phenomenal, just as the two higher planes are classed together as spiritual. They are essentially the worlds of phenomena, the worlds of concrete objects, the worlds in which forms are found with all their limitations; whereas the two higher are worlds which to the lower scrutiny are formless, in which the life is continually manifesting itself and moulding the subtle matter of those planes into immediate expression of itself. So that the great characteristic of the two higher regions is the manifestation of life, the great characteristic of the two lower the manifestation of form. Thus we may classify them in these pairs as phenomenal and spiritual.

When we come to deal with the mental world, the mânasic, we find that it partakes of the characteristics of those regions above and of those below, or, if we prefer to say so, of the inner and the outer. The lower half of the mental plane shows the distinct mark of the phenomenal worlds, the rûpa levels of form. And we notice that its phase of consciousness is that of the intellect, whose ideas are drawn from the phenomenal world and which takes sensations and feelings from that world below it, co-ordinates them, groups them together, draws its own conclusions from them, the whole of that work going on on the lower mental plane, that which we speak of as the levels of rûpa or form. Those levels, then, are distinctly related to the two lower worlds. But when we pass on to the higher, the upper half of the mental, we find that the intellect takes on the characteristics which belong to the higher regions or spiritual world. It is abstract, not concrete, in its character; it deals with ideas which from the stand-

point of the concrete intellect are formless, those
ideas that have the peculiar characteristic of existing in their own world as things perfectly intelligible, perfectly distinct, perfectly clear as seen by
the intuition of Manas, but that none the less, the
moment they pass on to the lower level of the mental plane, are found not to be one but many in
every case—one abstract idea belonging to the formless world giving birth perhaps to hundreds of concrete ideas, each one distinct with its own characteristic form. So that, looked at in this way, we see
that the mental plane seems to divide itself into
this dual relationship to the worlds above it and the
worlds below. Consciousness working thereon shows
out these two great characteristics—the concrete
dealing with the phenomenal, and the abstract reaching upwards toward the spiritual. This plane is essentially the human plane, it is the great battle-
ground of humanity; none of the combats that take
place on the physical or the astral planes are to be
compared in their intensity, in their importance, in
their subtlety, with the combats that are waged on
the mental plane. It is the plane of balance, the
plane having two below it and two above it, the
central plane for humanity, and in that sense the
most important and the most characteristic in human
evolution. It is there that the "I" develops, the
root and the centre of individuality; hence it is that

on this plane all the most terrible combats are waged. It is the place where success or failure comes to humanity in the course of our world evolution.

Now looking at the whole question in that rather wide way, trying to take, as it were, a bird's eye view of these planes on which human evolution is proceeding, we shall find, I think, that the question of consciousness will become very much easier to grasp. If we would understand the consciousness which is working on these planes, we must note the characteristics of each plane, and these will in turn be characteristics of the unconsciousness in its activity on any given plane; and the more we are able to recognize each of these planes as separate from the others, as having its own place in evolution, the more shall we be able to understand the workings of consciousness on each, the attributes which it will necessarily develop, the characteristics which it will inevitably show. And if we can work these out fairly, clearly and definitely, we shall not run into the danger of confusion into which I notice so many of our students do run, sometimes thinking that the emotional is the spiritual, and utterly misunderstanding the place of the mental in the total evolution of man.

There is one thing that we shall have to consider when we are dealing with consciousness, which does not at once come out clearly and plainly in this broad view that I have been taking. There is a kind of border-land between the astral and the mental planes; not a border-land in the sense of anything that intervenes between the two, but a region which is in a very real sense common to both; a region in which the higher matter of the astral plane and the lower matter of the mental plane work together in a peculiar and co-ordinated fashion, so that you cannot entirely separate them in their working, so that characteristics of both planes are there found to be united. And the product of activity, when the two kinds of matter from the higher astral and the lower mental are brought together and meet to work together, the product of that coalition has partly the intellectual stamp, partly the stamp which belongs to it as coming to it from the astral plane—the stamp of Kâma; so that we get a form of consciousness which we are obliged to distinguish by the term drawn from both, kâma-mânasic. And some of you, I daresay, in your studies, especially in reading the writings of H. P. Blavatsky, have sometimes been a little bit confused by this division which is brought in by her. So much does she bring it in, in fact, that she even occasionally speaks of the kâma-mânasic plane as a region where both Kâma and Manas are working together, where one cannot speak of it as wholly kâma or as wholly mânasic, where the two so interpenetrate each other that they may be separated from the pure workings of Manas on the one hand and of Kâma on the other, but where we get the characteristics of both. This region is therefore conveniently called by the names of both kâma-mânasic. The recognition of that will help us considerably in clearing up some of the difficulties that are left by the ordinary western division, between emotions, taken as divided into sensations and feelings, and the differences that arise between the different classes of feelings, which you will find in a moment that I shall prefer to separate off definitely as emotional.

One other point has to be considered before I take up these things separately, and it is this: that consciousness is one, and that however different the manifestations may be, the life within them is the same. There is but one life working in us, the life of Atmâ. It is that which, pouring forth from the nirvâṇic plane, presents itself as Buddhi on the buddhic plane, as Manas on the mânasic plane, as Kâma on the astral, as Prâna, through the etheric and the dense body, on the physical. There is but one life, no matter how different may be its manifestations; it is the essential consciousness, and that unit is the root of our being. Everything that is in us comes forth from that; and we should think of it as a great stream of outpouring energy, which changes its appearance and its colour as it clothes itself in the matter of one plane after another, the colour being lent it by the plane—the colouring matter, we might almost call it. While the essential life remains the same, remember always that that essential life draws into itself the colouring characteristic of any plane; so that when the evolution through all the planes is completed, the Atmâ has taken up the colouring of every plane, and is therefore very different at the conclusion of the human evolution from the Atmâ at the beginning of that evolution— a point which we are very often apt to lose sight of, and so to get a sort of despairing idea and to say of the whole evolution: "If it be Atmâ at the beginning and Atmâ at the ending, what has been done through all this pilgrimage?" While Atmâ may shake off all the matter of the planes, the colouring obtained through that matter is not lost.

Realizing this one outpouring energy, let us remember that in the course of evolution we have the mounting upwards, as the Monad climbs from the mineral to the vegetable, from the vegetable to the animal, from the animal to the animal-man; that we have the down-pouring stream, Atmâ-Buddhi-Manas, working downwards toward the mânasic plane, while Atmâ-Buddhi from below, as the Monad, is working upwards towards the mânasic plane. Hence that same central plane is the meeting-place of the two streams—another thing that shows us its enormous importance and the central position which I gave to it in the five as a whole. It is the meeting ground of the two great waves of evolution, the one going upwards from the second LOGOS, the other coming downwards from the First: they meet on the mental plane and there carry on what we may call the joint evolution.

Let us see, then, how emotion is to be distinguished, how it arises and how it manifests itself. We may here utilize quite rightly and quite fully the western psychology in the analysis that it gives of sensations and feelings. They belong to that upward-climbing Monad that we know as the wave from the second LOGOS, having the organizing characteristic of Atmâ-Buddhi climbing upwards in evolution. That climbing from the mineral to the vegetable begins, as we know, by the vivifying of astral matter, the Monad drawing it round itself for the purpose of expressing the capacity of what we call sensation. As it passes onwards from the vegetable to the animal, this astral matter is drawn very much more under the control of the Monad and is roughly shaped round it in the astral body of the animal, at which stage the characteristic of sensation becomes very marked.

Now what is sensation? It is the power to re-

spond to a stimulus from without, the response of
the organism to something that touches it, the answer which it sends out to that touch, the sensibility
to contact. We have learnt that this power of response resides in the astral matter, not in the physical, that the power of sensation is not a power which
is located in the physical body, but that all that the
physical body does is to provide certain organs
whereby stimuli may be sent in from the physical
world and conducted to the true centres of sensation in the astral body. If anything interferes with
the link between the astral and the physical, sensation stops; dislocate the astral from the physical,
and there is no sensation in the physical. As we
know in the use of various drugs, when that dis-
location is brought about we lose all power of sensation, of response to any stimulus that may touch
us from without. The power of sensation is in the
astral matter, and as that is aggregated together
into a primitive kind of astral body centres of sensation are gradually built up, and the animal feels,
responds to stimuli, and has what we call primary
sensations. As this astral body becomes better organized, these simple sensations aggregate themselves
together into feelings, very much after the fashion
that western psychology describes, and we have then
more complicated movements in the astral body
made up of a number of primary sensations, the

astral body adding to the mere response to the external stimulus its own power which has been evolved by way of those repeated responses. So that it gradually acquires, as it were, a kind of ready-made apparatus; an apparatus composed of a number of vibrations which are always ready to come into action as a group, and these aggregated vibrations we may at this stage call "feelings." They belong to the astral body, and they come as a great gush in answer to a stimulus, the impulse being in its nature the kind of sensation which gave rise within the astral body—by many repetitions and many workings of the astral body upon the sensation—to this feeling, which is then established as what we may call a group of vibrations; not the simple vibration of the answer that we call sensation, but the grouped, co-ordinated and modified vibrations which work together as a feeling.

Then comes the still further change which occurs when, from the mental plane, action takes place on the part of the awakened Manas, after the third life-wave has come down and Manas is brought into activity; that is mânasic matter is being brought together by that downward wave and the inchoate mental body is formed. We then find that this mental matter begins to vibrate when the astral matter is set vibrating very vehemently, and that when these complicated groups of vibrations are active in

the astral body, an answering vibration is set up in
the growing mental body. That vibration lends to
the feeling something of the mental character. Then
memory comes in, and a little inclination to reason
and to judgment, and so on; a certain intellectual
quality is thus imparted to the feeling, which en-
riches and deepens it and tends to make it more permanent, giving it a more defined character of its
own. This separates it off still more distinctly from
other groups of feelings, or vibrations that are
called feelings, in its turn; and this mental quality,
which is due to the mental region inter-working
with the astral, gives us what I will define as emotion. So that we now have three classes instead of
the two of western psychology which takes emotion
as the whole. I am taking sensation, feeling and
emotion as a triad, as three classes which can be distinguished the one from the other; the first two, the
sensations and the feelings, being really kâmic or
astral, the third, emotion, being kâma-mânasic—the
Manas and Kâma both entering into it and producing this kâma-mânasic vibration. This, in order to
use an ordinary English word, we will speak of as
"emotion," remembering that its distinguishing mark
is this mental, this intellectual touch added to that
of Kâma.

It will probably make these theoretical distinctions, as we may perhaps call them, a little clearer

if I take two illustrations. One, which you would generally characterize—when you bring morality into the question—as good, and the other which you would characterize—regarded from the moral standpoint—as bad. Certain sensations in primitive man, as in the animal, are pleasurable, others painful. Take the group of pleasurable sensations which arise either in the animal or in animal-man in contact with another animal or animal-man of the opposite sex—I am using the word man, of course, in the double sense. Where there is sex difference, the coming into touch with each other gives rise, at the earliest possible stage, to a certain feeling of mutual attraction, a feeling which will be called pleasurable in its nature and which attracts the two together. It is nothing more than a response of the nature of sensation on the part of each to the stimulus afforded by the other; but the two opposites that run all through the universe and that express themselves as sex on the physical plane—when they come towards each other embodied in two forms separated for the time, attract each other. Each acts as a stimulus to the other and there is the stimulus giving rise to a sensation; but it is a complete interaction, each acting as a stimulus to the opposite, each feeling the sensation in reply to that stimulus. Here there is nothing but the simple sensation in the most primitive form. After a time, however, the

activity of the astral body, the grouping together
of many such sensations and the placing them, as
it were, in connection with beings that have the
characteristics of the opposite sex, give rise to a
feeling which we may then characterize as something
more than a mere sexual sensation. We might call
it passion, still animal whether in the brute or in the
animal-man, but distinguishable from mere sensation,
less primitive in its character, with a great deal
more astral force and life coming into it. So that
the consciousness—which, remember, is a unit—responding by this far more highly organized astral
grouping, will have far more complicated vibrations;
and these we may speak of as sexual passion. Then
comes the time when the intelligence begins to work
in connection with this passion, when the intelligence
begins to bring in its finer and keener vibrations and
we have the emotion of love, kâma-mânasic in its
character. Later there will be a recognition of many
other elements that should enter into that passion
to purify and to refine it, and all sorts of other ideas
will come into connection with it—the ideas of sacrifice and self-surrender and the helpfulness and desire to make happy—and then the whole feeling is
enriched and purified and elevated by this influx
of the intelligence working in the mental body. In
this survey we get the three stages: the sensation,
which is the mere response to the stimulus from the

opposite sex; the passion, which is the more complicated feeling and into which very many more vibrations in the astral bodies enter; and the emotion,
love, of a far higher character and containing far
loftier possibilities. These, speaking generally, would
be on the side that we should call good.

Then, if we study the question on the side that
we regard as evil, we may take a similar step of three
stages in connection with pain. Pain is caused by
two antagonists meeting each other, when their
meeting gives rise, say by a blow inflicted by one
on the other, to a sensation of pain—a response from
the astral body, unpleasant, inharmonious, troublesome in its character. That, as a simple sensation,
would be nothing more than pain. But gradually
that passes, being connected with the one who inflicted the pain, into what we may call the passion
of resentment, and the astral body feels an impulse
to return the pain it has received; and this passion
of resentment, looked at from the standpoint merely
of the pairs of opposites, is the corresponding cor-
relative of the passion of attraction on the other side.
Then, passing on to the time when the intelligence
begins to touch this feeling, or passion, of resentment, we have hatred evolved, just the opposite of
love, the repulsion against attraction, that also belonging to the kâma-mânasic region. Hatred is an
emotion, not simply a feeling, having this intellect-

ual quality which has deepened and enriched it and made it keener and more subtle in its nature, capable of giving rise to other vibrations exceedingly destructive in their character, just as those given rise to by the vibrations of the emotion of love are constructive in their character. For here we have indeed one of those great pairs of opposites which are working throughout the whole of the universe.

These two illustrations will probably enable you to bear in mind, in somewhat concrete fashion, what I mean—whether I am defining them rightly is a matter for debate—by these three classes of sensations, passions and emotions, or sensations, feelings— if you like to use that word instead of passions— and emotions. Now coming from that to an analysis of the action of consciousness on the intellectual, the mental plane, we shall find that its working takes on an entirely different character, that there are certain broad lines of division which separate off its experiences as mânasic from its experiences as kâmic.

First of all, if you look at the kâmic experiences broadly, you will find that they are all of the nature of rushing outwards, that they are all pouring themselves out to seek, that they are never satisfied by an expression which is contained within the consciousness—which is a feeling—but that consciousness is always trying to reach outwards to something

which it looks at as external to itself. That is a
broad characteristic of the whole of those—whether
you take sensation, or passion, or emotion, it does
not matter—they are all marked by this common
peculiarity, that they are all part of the outward-
rushing energy of Atmâ; they rush outwards to
seek expression and satisfaction in the phenomenal
world, they cannot be satisfied alone. In fact, if we
think for a moment, we cannot imagine any of those
things as existing alone; if we could think of a person as perfectly isolated in the universe, this out-
ward-rushing energy would be stopped; it could not
express itself except in connection with another.
That is the great mark of action on the kâmic plane,
and it is a mark of enormous importance if you want
to understand some of the problems I alluded to at
the beginning.

But now, when we come to deal with the mental
plane, we are at once struck with this immense difference—that it is self-contained. When the consciousness begins to work in its intellectual aspect,
and to work with pure mânasic matter undisturbed
by these astral vibrations—leaving out the kâma-
mânasic entirely—it draws itself in, it concentrates
itself, it endeavours to shut out the external world,
and looks on everything that comes from outside as
a disturbing influence which prevents it from con-
centrating itself and from exercising its faculties in

the natural way. So that the very first thing that the consciousness will do when it begins to work on the mental plane will be to draw itself inwards, carrying with it that with which it has come into contact on the astral plane. It cannot get ideas until it draws in from the astral body a large number of those emotions which grow out of the feelings and sensations on the astral plane, and which have been worked up in the astral body and have been handed on by it, for the next activity, to the mental plane. All the great ideas with which that consciousness is going to work will be drawn from the sensations which have been obtained by the astral body coming into contact with the outer universe. There, again, western psychology is right; it is continually right in its earlier analysis, while it breaks down when it comes to deal with the deeper phases of consciousness. It is quite true that when dealing with the awakening mentality in man everything is found to depend upon what is supplied to it from outside: it cannot start itself, it must answer; and the earlier vibrations of the mânasic consciousness can only be awakened by receiving vibrations from outside which shall stir it into activity. It will then send out a little answer, and as it sends it out it will draw back again, drawing with it the experiences it has obtained; but it cannot make any use of those experiences outside its own limits, it can do nothing with them as mental food, until it draws them within the circle of the mind and begins then to work upon them in its own sphere. And in order to do that successfully, having drawn itself in, it must shut out the external world and must not permit all these surging vibrations to come in and confuse its attention, for its attention has to be directed to that which it has drawn into itself, if it is to make any use of those experiences and so develop germinal intellectual faculties. Bear in mind, then, this fundamental difference of intellectual working. True, it must gather from outside, the astral body must hand on; but the condition of success for the intellectual working is that it shall concentrate itself on that which is obtained from the lower vehicle. Drawing in these results, these threads, it sets to work upon them, and all its characteristic workings are these internal vibrations which deal with the fruits of the experience gathered from outside. It puts side by side a number of these things which we call at this stage "perceptions," and these perceptions or percepts are ranged side by side, and the mind contemplates them and begins to develop what we call the power of comparison. Looking at them all, it sees their likeness and their differences and compares one with another. Having thus considered and compared them, it begins to draw out their likenesses and puts those likenesses together and

out of them forms an idea of a rather more elaborate
character: it then takes all the differences and makes
those into dividing marks. We find now an immense
amount of what we call analysis—that is, the breaking up of these things by the comparison which recognizes identities and differences; and by fixing the
attention on differences the process of analysis goes
on.

Thus the mind, in its lower stages, by taking all
these concrete ideas which it evolves from all that it
has obtained from the outer world, by putting them
together and classifying them, by building up more
complicated ideas of them, develops, by means of
this concrete activity, all the powers that we recognize as the intellectual powers—judgment, reasoning, comparison, memory, then the drawing of conclusions, the deductive and inductive faculties, the
logical faculties—all these things are gradually
evolved. But if we consider them, we shall see that
their evolution must depend on the power of the
mind to isolate itself, so that it shall not be confused
by inrushes from the outer world. It wants to be
alone, it wants to be quiet, it wants to shut the doors
of the senses, and within its own self-contained realm
to apply itself to those results which it has obtained
from the lower vehicles in which the consciousness
has been functioning. It is only as this has gone on
to a very great extent, as the phenomenal world has

been used for the shaping of all these concrete ideas and the working upon them and the reasoning upon them, it is only then that the higher faculties of the intelligence will begin to evolve on the formless planes, and abstract thought—the drawing out of the common element in these various separated concrete ideas—will begin. Slowly and gradually that lower activity will make active the Higher Manas; on its own plane it will enter on its especial work of abstract thinking, and the highest intellectual faculties will then be gradually developed. These higher faculties are classified as synthetical rather than as analytical: they are no longer engaged in breaking up into their component parts the ideas on which the mental activity has been working, but are re-combing them and by synthesis are creating new ideas— ideas which are the images of realities in the Universal Mind. This is the quality in man which makes it possible that he in turn shall become universal, which evolves within the limits of the causal body that third aspect of the life of the first LOGOS, that quality of the Universal Mind which is to be the essence of individuality when the limits of the individual have fallen away.

Looking at that, then, as a rough definition of mental working, we come back again to the idea which is so important for our understanding of its place in evolution, that the mind is the self-contained part of

the consciousness, and that the self-containing is necessary for its perfect evolution. The mental plane
is, as we have seen, the balance, the centre of the
whole evolution. The plane above and the plane below have a certain definite relation the one to the
other, and this relation lies in the common characteristic that in both of them is the consciousness
pouring itself out. On the buddhic plane the consciousness is pouring itself outwards; on the kâmic
plane the consciousness is also pouring itself outwards. In both cases it is seeking expression by unifying. On the kâmic plane it does this on a much
lower level by gaining possession of an object and
bringing it into itself, by taking possession of it as
"mine," by holding it and assimilating it; whereas
on the higher plane, the buddhic, it pours itself
forth to include, and not feeling the sense of difference, of the "I" and of the "mine," it is conscious of a unity which sees all that it touches as
part of itself and includes all within itself. Thus
the outpouring differs in this subtle way from the
outpouring on the kâmic plane, that the one is pouring out to the external, while the other, if I may
use the phrase, is pouring internally. The consciousness on the higher plane recognizes everything as
part of its own life and its own nature; it does not
need to go forth in order to find, finding all as
within itself, yet still having that expansive char-

acter which is continually including, never excluding, which does not know limitations, which does
not recognize boundaries. Hence it has sometimes
been said that the kâmic plane is the reflection of
the buddhic on a lower level; it shows, as it were,
in an image down below a kind of reflection of the
qualities which are found above. Just as may be
seen in the water the reflection of a mountain which
is by the side of a lake, so in Kâma there is a kind
of reflection of certain buddhic qualities. And thinking, as we are taught to think, of the whole of these
creative activities as pairs continually reflected, we
find these pairs existing on the nirvânic and the
physical planes, on the buddhic and the kâmic, and
once more the intellectual region as the point of
balance for the whole.

Now this, if carefully worked out in our thought,
will throw considerable light upon those curious
problems that I spoke of with regard to the wonderful and unexpected change that sometimes takes
place in the life of an individual, with regard also
to that problem as to why we find a touch of deeper
insight in some who—especially in old age after a
life of unselfishness and of compassion—are able to
give us counsel and advice marked by that deeper
insight which we are accustomed to connect with
the idea of spiritual activity. Let us think of the
change itself. We find, perhaps, a person in whom

the rush of the emotional nature is tremendously strong; he is marked by great enthusiasm, by a headlong quality, by lack of balance, by lack of considcration, by a tendency to rush with enormous energy into some undertaking which attracts the feelings and the emotions. Perhaps it is some scheme of benevolence which may be exceedingly ill-considered, which may have in it innumerable flaws and blunders, all of which will work mischief as that scheme of benevolence is put into activity. But the strong emotional nature has no time to think of that; the tremendous surge of emotion carries it right away and it only sees that the scheme promises to do good, promises to end misery, to sweep away poverty, to change the face of the world. It cannot stop for all the cold consideration as to whether means are adapted to ends, and all the rest; it must go out in a tremendous rush, and out it goes. It does a considerable amount of good, and also a very large amount of evil; it breaks down a great many things that might have helped, it gives life to a great many things that are bitter exceedingly; and the whole thing is a great wave—with all the force of a wave certainly—but also with the destructive power which ill-regulated force must always present. It destroys, truly, but yet has within it that great constructive force of the universe, the emotion of love, the desire to help. In that outrush, therefore, it is also con-

structing, and having in it that quality of love, it
brings about a certain answering vibration on the
buddhic plane. By the self-surrender that will continually go with that great onrush of emotion and
enthusiasm, by the willingness of the person who
feels it to throw his own life away if only he may
serve the larger life that he sees suffering around
him, by the great impulse of self-sacrifice that does
not count the cost but is willing to give itself completely—health and life and everything else—if only
the suffering be relieved, is added to the kâmic passion and emotion a touch from the buddhic plane,
some recognition of the unity which makes it seem
well that the separated life should give itself for
the life of the whole. Thus is set stirring within the
evolving life, the evolving Self, a little vibration,
from the buddhic plane which will throw down on to
the kâmic a slight ray of light, giving to it its own
beauty and attractive power and working in him
who feels it, however ill-considered his action, however foolish that which he does, for the evolution of
the spiritual nature and thus enabling a step forward to be made in that incarnation. The light
from the buddhic plane, thrown upon the intelligence, brings it also into greater activity, enables it
to see an idea of which, when intellectually recognized, the intellect takes hold. The intellect seizes
this great force which was started in the kâmic na-

ture, changes its direction, while leaving it as a force, and utilizes that tremendous energy, directing it to a wiser end and by a wiser method, so that the whole nature evolves forwards and upwards and a great change is seen even within the limits of one life.

For it must be remembered that for progress force is absolutely necessary and that force is continually being evolved by way of the emotions. Granted that in the earlier stages of that emotional rush it may be a force which is working very foolishly, none the less is it a force; whereas if there is no force there is not the motive-power which will get the creature on. He lacks the steam, and however perfect the machine, it will not go if there is no steam in it. We may have a piece of magnificent machinery which, if we could set it going, might do wonders; but if we cannot get any steam into the boiler, or if the boiler is too small to give sufficient energy for the moving of the machine, it will remain there without motion for want of that energy that should come from its boiler. Now the kâmic nature is the boiler of the evolving Self, and no machinery that it can make anywhere, however admirable it may be and whatever its possibilities in the future, can work in any given incarnation if that force which will move it is lacking. But given the force, we can turn it to any end that is recognized as good; and when the

gleam of buddhic light shines down upon the intelligence, that illuminated intelligence will recognize a great ideal and will begin to utilize the force
and turn it in a better direction. A change in the
object is all that is needed in these cases. Turn the
same force towards a higher object and the aim will
be achieved. The great force in the kâmic nature
that was being used for the sake of the personal
self, when turned to the service of the common Self
of man will make the hero, the pioneer and the
saint. It is a change in the direction of the force
caused by the change of the object which is recognized as desirable: make that change—and it is sometimes done by a flash of illumination—and then the
whole of that energy will be turned towards the
achieving of the higher end.

Suppose, however, that there is a great development of the pure intellect only, while this emotional
side of the nature has been dwarfed and stunted in
any given incarnation; or suppose that in the course
of evolution the tendency has been especially towards
the intellectual, while the emótional nature life after
life has been little developed—which is quite possible, because our development is often exceedingly
lop-sided—there will then be building on the mental
plane a piece of magnificent machinery that in a
future incarnation will be of priceless value. Do not
imagine for one moment that its building is to be

deprecated; do not imagine that it is to be considered
undesirable; it is necessary for the full and per-
feet evolution, it has to be made at some time or
another, it has gradually to be achieved in one incarnation or another, but I am simply considering
one incarnation for the sake of clearing the mind.
Imagine, then, that the whole of it has been devoted
to the intellectual building — towards analysis,
towards synthesis, towards working out ideas on the
mental plane—what is the end of that working? Isolation. We build round us a wall to keep the outer
impacts away, trying to be calm and still and un-
touched by anything from outside, in order that the
mental energy, balanced naturally, may do its work.
There we have the building up of the great mânasic
possibilities; but such a nature may find in any one
incarnation insuperable difficulties in the way of
achieving the spiritual life. The isolation is that
which makes the very expansion which is a necessity
of the spiritual life impossible for the time, and the
whole conditions of the working are those which are
least favourable to the expansive and inclusive qualities. And although such a life would have a most
useful and necessary place in the total evolution—
as bringing the intellect into magnificent working
order and ensuring a splendid and rapid evolution
in a future birth, yet, for the time being, spiritual
aid would be practically thrown away upon it, be-

cause the whole force of the evolution would be turned towards the concentrated, isolated growth,/ and not towards the pouring forth of life.

Now in looking at the whole of our nature in this way, we shall see how necessary the evolution of each of the planes is for the perfect growth, the perfect expression of the Self. We shall see how, instead of putting the one against the other—the intellectual man decrying the emotional, and the emotional man saying hard things about the intellectual, the one scornfully saying that it is only cold intellect, and the other saying, with equal scorn, that it is only ill-regulated emotion—the balanced and thoughtful person would see in each a necessary stage of evolution and, if he had reached the point where he was able to give help to each, would consider only the nature of the aid that he should give, in order to help forward a man to the best possible advantage in the activities to which the Self in him was chiefly turning its attention. For we continually fail to recognize that it is the Self in each of us that should be the guiding force in our evolution; that it is not for one to say how the Self in another shall evolve, what activities he shall develop in one incarnation, what line he shall follow in any particular birth. The Self itself chooses the pathway along which it will go, and it is for that inner Self to decide for its vehicles which of them it will develop, along which path lies for it the line of least resistance in any given birth. And anyone who, having evolved to a higher life, is able to help those who have not reached so far, will not consider which qualities to him may be most attractive, which path to him may seem most intrinsically desirable; he will rather consider what the Self is working out in that individual and how he can bring energy to bear to assist the Self in its work in that incarnation which it has in hand. So that in all the dealings of the great Masters with evolving humanity, this question of means and methods, of times and seasons, exercises determining force on the nature of the help They give; and many people would sometimes feel less discouraged, would, in their judgment of the great work which goes on around them, be better balanced and would be seeing things more clearly, if they recognised that the Master gives help in the way that it is most needed by the individual, and does not think for one moment whether in giving that help its nature may be misconstrued, or whether He may be thought to be more or less generous in His contact with any particular soul. He gives what He knows to be the best; He does not give what might bring Him the greatest outrush of gratitude from the limited consciousness with which He is dealing. It often happens, therefore, that in dealing with a man of keen intellect, of great mental power, the Master gives help which is never appreciated by that man during the whole of his incarnation. He helps him onward in his intellectual growth, helps him to strengthen and to build more perfectly his intellectual apparatus, not minding at all, in His perfect selflessness, in His perfect compassion, whether the man, if he knows of the Master's existence, may think himself neglected, unhelped, or left on one side; but giving, as all Those do give Who stand on those heights of selflessness, the exact aid which is wanted by the evolving Self to quicken its evolution, the exact kind of succour which makes the final achievement easier than it would otherwise be.

I cannot but think that if, as students, we were sometimes to look at the matter in this broader way, dealing with it in the light of Theosophical knowledge, we should become more compassionate, more tolerant, more charitable to the infinite diversity of evolution that we see around us on every side; more able to help our brothers, more grateful for the help that we ourselves receive.

On Moods

Reprinted from "The Theosophical Review" for November, 1904.

As we all know in theory, the Theosophical Society has as its work in the world the spreading of the great truths of the WISDOM, and most of us believe the facts that these truths are preserved to the world, generation after generation, by the great body of spiritual Teachers whom we speak of as the White Lodge. Those Teachers have their claim on our allegiance because They are the greatest servants of humanity. They stand out above and beyond all other Helpers of men by the immensity of Their sacrifice for the sake of the world, and by the perfection with which Their service is rendered. It is not too much to say of Them that Their very existence lies in sacrifice. Great as are the interests with which They deal, far-reaching as is the wisdom with which They scan the worlds and the evolution of humanity, none the less we know—as all of us have been told and some of us have observed—that despite that immense width of work and of duty They are in fullest and tenderest sympathy with the individual efforts of individual men and women. To us, of course, it is well-nigh impossible to realise how comprehension so vast is at the same time so minute in its observation. We ourselves, as our interests widen, are so apt to become more careless of details, are so apt to look on the smaller things of life as though they were insignificant. We are not yet at that point of greatness which is able to look on all things we call great or small as neither small nor great—that point of greatness which considers the perfection with which work may be done as far more important than the importance of the work in the eyes of the world. It is difficult for us, because we are not yet great, to understand this bringing together of points that to us seem to be so opposite in their nature; and yet it is one of the profoundest truths in the universe that the greater the comprehension the more complete, tender and sympathetic is the attention to detail, is the feeling with all that breathes. Greater in range of vision most certainly is the Logos of our system than the Masters who serve under His direction, and yet even closer than Their touch with Their disciples is His touch with all. Literally and perfectly true is that phrase spoken by the Christ that "Not a sparrow falleth to the ground without your Father." To that all-embracing Love and Life

all lives which are a part of Itself are infinitely dear
and precious. In the immensity of the Mind which
comprehends and supports them all, every distinction disappears, so that that phrase of the poet:

Closer is He than breathing, nearer than hands and feet,

is literally true of the LOGOS of our universe. And
true is it also that They in whom His spirit is more
manifest than it is in us, alike in the extent of Their
knowledge and in the deepness and detail of Their
sympathy, are more like Him than we are like Them.

But while this is true, the great Ideal that They
present to us is surely one which we may well endeavour to some extent to reproduce in our lives;
for just in proportion as we can extend our knowledge, and deepen, refine and make sensitive our
emotions, so are we gradually evolving along the
line which at last shall bring us closer to Their perfection. And in this article I wish to urge the infinite importance to each one of us, as member of
the Theosophical Society, as member of the nation
or the home, of trying to join together and to evolve
in our own life these two aspects of the far-reaching
and the detailed sensitive and tender feeling towards
each. In the proportion that we reach the Wisdom.
which is the realisation of the One Life, so als
must be the proportion in which we manifest the
Love, which is the unity of that Wisdom manifesting itself in the diversity of forms; for just as Wis-

dom recognises that all lives are one, so does the
separate life—realising that Wisdom and yet the infinite variety of separate forms—try to draw its
own enveloping form towards the other envelopes
of the Soul. The drawing together of the forms by
the Life is that which we know as Love; so that the
Wisdom of the buddhic plane is the Love of the
emotional plane. And as that Wisdom begins to
bud on the higher plane its aspect in our emotions
must flower in proportion. It is this recognition in
our own lives of the duty of knowing, and of the
duty of loving, which builds up that rounded perfection of character after which each one of us
should strive. In the past we have naturally evolved
perhaps strongly in the direction of knowledge or
strongly in the direction of love and sympathy. It
is our duty, now that we are beginning to understand things better, to take our emotions into our
own hands and our evolution under our own control;
that we should see that these two things that seem
so different down here are really but two aspects
of the same Life as manifested on the higher planes
of being. And as we see this intellectually and try
to realise it emotionally, we shall be developing the
type of character which approaches to the possibility of Initiation into the Higher Life, we shall be
preparing ourselves for that growth of wisdom which

makes possible the opening of our eyes on the budd- /
hic plane.

Now, one great obstacle that we find in our way,
both with regard to the growth of our knowledge
and to the refining and deepening of our emotions,
is the obstacle of changeableness in ourselves, that
which we sometimes speak of as our changing moods.
And these are very curious and strange: curious,
because they seem to alter our whole attitude towards the very things of which really our certainty
is the most profound; strange, because of the enormous power which they wield over us. On what
we call an April day, when clouds and sunshine are
rapidly suceeding one another, we see a landscape at
one moment dark, then bright; then a portion shines
out brightly while another portion is clouded, and
so on; as the clouds and sunshine change so the
whole appearance of things, either shadowed or illuminated, alters; the stream which shines like silver
in the sunlight rolls grey and dull beneath the cloud.
We see these changes and we know that they are
due to the clouds and the sunrays succeeding one
another in relation to these things, so that the relation between them is that which changes and makes
the immense difference in appearance. And so with
us. These moods which have immense power over
us, which influence us so profoundly, are the changing clouds and sunshine of the intellectual and the

emotional temperaments—it is chiefly to the emotional temperament that these changing moods must
be traced. For although it is perfectly true that so
far as the intellect is concerned it is sometimes alert
and sometimes sluggish, sometimes quick to grasp
and sometimes slow, sometimes inclined to labour
and sometimes to be idle, those changes are really
not of the essence of the intellectual nature at all,
but only that of the intellectual nature as it works
beneath the clouds or sunshine that come to it by
contact with the emotional plane. When we want
to deal with these moods which sweep over us we
must trace them to their origin in the region of the
emotions, and learn how they can be dealt with
there.

I put side by side the moods of sunshine and of
cloud because the sunshiny condition is quite as
much a mood as the cloudy one—they go together, a
pair of opposites, and if we watch ourselves, we
find that just in proportion to the depth and completeness of the depression of one time is the brightness and completeness of the sunshiny mood of another. People who do not sink low in depression
do not rise high in elation, while those who at one
time are in a state of brilliant delight are those who
at another sink down to the very depths of depression. It is a question of the swing of the emotions,
and, just as in the swing of a pendulum, the further

it swings one side the further it will swing on the other side of the middle point, so it is also with our emotions. Now this is one of the marked peculiarities of western peoples, and we have it very largely from being born in western nations. For it is a very marked peculiarity that as we travel eastwards this great changeability of moods largely disappears—not entirely, but so much so that it is scarcely perceptible when one is accustomed to the immense changes which sweep over the western nature, and it is a point which I have often observed during my stay in India. I have found it has been for myself a matter of difficulty and continued struggle to reach the kind of equability of mood which seems almost the natural condition of the ordinary cultivated Indian mind. I do not, of course, know at all intimately the people of other eastern nations, but I should imagine from much that I have heard that this equability is also found among the people on the other side of the Indian Peninsula.

This equability of mood is an immense advantage; it prevents a person from being thrown continually off his feet either in one direction or another, and if he is devoted to any particular ideal at one time, you may expect to find him devoted to that when you meet him perhaps at long intervals. We, on the other hand, continually find that our attitude changes, so far as our emotions are concerned, to our ideals. And our moods change not only with reference to our ideals; I should like also to pause for a moment on certain moods which come to us that do not affect us so deeply, in order to clear them out of the way and distinguish them from the more important moods.

Now, first of all, we have a certain amount of changeability of moods caused by the nerves. Very often depression or elation, irritability or calm, are matters very largely dependent on the state of the physical nerves. And those who are students of their own nature should try to divide off the moods of that kind from those of a more serious nature. These things are to be conquered, to be got rid of definitely by a certain amount of reasonableness, common-sense and understanding. First we must separate them from the others; we must see how far our nervous condition is at the root of our changing moods—a little extra tension of the nerves, a little extra fatigue, a little loss of sleep, will make all the difference in this type of moods. When we recognise that for responsible beings it is a thing of which to be ashamed, we should try to get beyond them by endeavouring to keep our bodies as healthy as possible, a duty to ourselves and to those around us; if the body is out of sorts then necessarily, unless we are very strong, there will be this nervous reaction in our moods. We may be strong enough to prevent it; we cannot be strong enough to work against it as if the nerves were in good order. And one necessity is the deliberate measuring of our strength and fitting what we do to that measure. It is not a question of the amount of work, but of the proportion between the amount of work and our ability to do it; the amount of work one can do will be different from what another can do, and it is no use to judge by the amount of work; we must judge the power of the person to do the work without being thrown into an overstrained condition. There is where common-sense and wisdom come in. My own rule for marking out my work is simply to see how much out of all the claims upon me I can attend to, knowing what power I have at my disposal; and when I have marked that out, I do not go outside it, no matter how much people may blame me for not doing what they think I ought to do in attending to them—and that is often difficult, because it wants a certain amount of grim determination, when you have marked out what you have to do, not to let yourself be forced beyond. Yet this is the right way for the Wisdom-student to act, not only because he has no right to break down in the service he is offering to his Master, but because it is not "duty" to do more than we are able to do, and that which is not duty is beating the air. That is an important lesson in occult teaching: we cannot effectively do more than it is our duty to do; if we try to do more, everything outside the duty is so much wasted time and work; it is mere folly to try to do it. There is also the great fact that by doing what is not our duty, we are preventing someone else from doing what is his duty, merely out of our own conceit. We often overstrain ourselves because we think we are the only people who can do this work. As a matter of fact there are many other people who can do it. This lesson in occult economy is one I recommend to all who are apt to over-strain themselves and break down. It is a blunder in practice, and hinders the evolution of those around us; they must evolve as well as we, and we have no right to take away from them their fair opportunities of growth by service. These overstrained nerves from overwork are things that should be looked on as absolutely wrong.

Let us put aside that sort of mood, and take another kind, which is very often distressing, but would be less so if rightly understood. I mean, those that come from our increasing sensitiveness to super-physical conditions, before we are sufficiently evolved to recognise what those influences are. As we evolve our astral bodies, they not only receive more impressions from the astral plane but pass them on more to the physical body, and so we find a mood of great depression coming over us for which we cannot in any way account. Now very often such a mood is simply an overshadowing from the astral plane with which we have really no more to do ourselves than the stream which is shadowed by the cloud has directly to do with the cloud. These clouds come over us from the astral plane, sometimes because one we love at a distance is suffering, sometimes because some misfortune is on its way to us and the shadow foreruns it—we have seen and felt it on the astral plane before it comes into view on the physical. Sometimes it is that there are troubles not of those immediately connected with us but of those in our neighbourhood, setting up some vibrations to which we unconsciously and sympathetically respond, and the wider our sympathies the more liable to depressions of this kind we are. People, for instance, who feel strongly about public matters, who are deeply interested in the welfare of large numbers of their fellow men, such people would feel a very heavy depression sometimes from public calamities which are impending or going on at the time. Take, for instance, such a thing as the trouble caused by a great strike. Many people who do not suffer directly from it, who are not in themselves physically suffering directly, might get clouds of depression coming over them from the actual sufferings of the people under depression at the time,

and so with many public events either coming or
present.

What, then, can a person do when a mood of this
sort comes along? The only way I know of meeting
those is by the clear, definite recognition of the law;
the feeling that nothing can come to us or to others
which is not within the law, the feeling that whatever comes is working to a good purpose and for a
good end, the intense inner conviction that just as
when a trouble comes and we see it and understand
it we deliberately train ourselves to accept it and
live through it, so we are to deal with these vaguer
and obscurer things. We need not let the vagueness
overpower us; we should not let the obscurity blind
us to the working of the law, and we should habitually cultivate the frame of mind which faces everything that may come with fearlessness, remembering
that great truth written in an eastern scripture:
"Brahman is fearless," and those who share His
nature should also share His fearlessness. The cul-
tivation of a spirit that is without fear is one of the
very best things any one of us can do; to face the
world knowing it is full of cloud and sunshine, and
to be willing to pass through each in turn, refusing
when the feeling of depression comes to let it master
us, recognising it as a shadow thrown upon us from
outside, and declining to allow that shadow to influence the light that is within. That clear recog-

nition that many of the clouds of depression are
simply from the astral plane, the dealing with them
as impulses that affect us from that region, the looking at them in this light, calmly and deliberately,
will generally remove them from our path, and
make them take their proper place as simply interesting psychological facts which we do not permit to
disturb or affect our serenity.

These, then, are what I may call the less important moods: those that come from the nervous system, and those that come down upon us from the
astral region. And all of you who are anxious to
become more sensitive and to develop the inner
psychical faculties, might consider, when dealing
with these moods of depression, how, if you are affected by them, you would face the things which are
casting these shadows; how, say, physical life would
be carried on, if you had continually in mind all
these incidents on the astral plane which in the
mere shadow cast down on the waking consciousness
have so much power to depress; because until you
have grown entirely beyond being affected by such
moods, until you have got rid of that lack of con-
fidence in the law which makes it possible for these
to affect you so strongly, it is better that your eyes
should remain closed. It would be impossible for
you to have a moment's peace or quiet, if that wider
life pressed upon you, and if you could see on the

one side all its troubles with the wondering how to meet them, and on the other all its joys with the inevitable elation and impatience that those joys would bring.

Passing from the less important to the more important moods, what is it in us which at one time makes us full of enthusiasm and at another quite indifferent? Why, to put it plainly, at one time does our theosophical work appear to us as the one thing that makes life worth living and at another (if we speak perfectly honestly to ourselves) we do not care a bit about it, we have neither love for it nor wish to be in it. I know that is a strong way of putting it, but I do not think it is too strong; I have felt this myself time after time. It is a hard and difficult mood to be in, mostly because it is a mood that makes people think they have gone suddenly back in evolution, or made some tremendous failure; it is nothing of the kind, and what is more, these feelings of not caring for, or of indifference towards, our ideals are not of themselves of any importance. What is important is our conduct under them; what we *feel* does not matter much, how we *act* under the sway of the feelings matters immensely, and that is the real test of enthusiasm. Do we, when we do not care, act exactly as if we did? Are we strong enough, when we feel that everything is dead, to go on exactly as if everything were pulsing with

the most vivid life? Can we work as strenuously,
serve as completely, devote ourselves as utterly, when
the ideal is dim and vague as when it is brilliant and
filling our life with light? If we can do this, our
devotion is worth something; if we cannot, there is
still much to learn. And that is one of the thoughts
I would like to arouse in all of us, because these
changes of mood are not possible to escape until we
have risen very high. I do not know, in fact, how
high it is necessary to rise in order to get quite
beyond those stages in which the attitude in feeling
to the ideal appears to change.

And how shall we meet these moods? First, I
think, by a recognition of what is called the law
of rhythm, which H. P. B., in *The Secret Doctrine*,
puts as one of the fundamental truths; and yet it
is a law which few people understand at all, apparently, in its bearing on themselves. What are
these moods of enthusiasm and indifference but the
inevitable working of this law of periodicity? These
moods must take their part in our emotional and
intellectual life—as inevitably as night and day, as
necessary as night and day. A person who was
without these changes would be like a person who
was either always in the night or always in the
day. But the wise man should endeavour to bring
the day into the night and the night into the day,
and that brings about what is often called the

Higher Indifference, an equability that is maintained under all conditions. It is not that the night and day cease to follow each other; it is not that the darkness and light do not still fall upon the soul; but that the soul, recognising them, is no longer affected by them, feels them without being shaken by them, experiences them without confusing them with himself.

We shall recognise then this law of periodicity, that the changes will come, and we shall be ready to meet them. When the mood of indifference comes, we will quietly say to ourselves: "I was very enthusiastic for a considerable time; necessarily now I must feel the reverse." The moment we are able to say that and think it, the power of the darkness over us lessens; the darkness is there as before, but we have separated ourselves from it; we see it as an external thing which does not flood the recesses of the soul, we realise it as something belonging to the lower, changing, astral body. And by that very act of separation, by the recognition of the law that is working and that is good in its working, we remember the day in the darkness of the night, and we remember the darkness of night in the day. Some people do not care to remember the darkness during the period of light. But if they want to gain power over both they must do so . They must check the mood of over-elation quite as much as the mood of over-depression. The mood of lightness is more dangerous than the mood of darkness; it contains more perils, for it is just in the time when we feel most elated that we do the things that afterwards we wish we had not done, and lose that vigilance which the pressure of the darkness makes us maintain. The sentry is less careful in the light than in the night-time, and sometimes, therefore, more easily surprised. Most of the slips we make are in the time of brightness rather than in the time of darkness. Understanding the law of rhythm, then, is the first step towards becoming master of our moods.

The next step is the intellectual one, which definitely recognises that the ideal which is beautiful at one time must be beautiful still, although its charm for us may have vanished. That which is beauty cannot cease to be beauty because our eyes are blinded. We shall bring the clear light of the intellect to bear on the clouds, we shall realise that that which, when our sight was clear, was seen to be good is good, no matter what clouds may sweep around it. And just as the mariner takes his bearings by the sun and by the stars when he is able to see them because they are not covered by clouds, but steers by these bearings afterwards when the clouds have covered the sky, so should we, when the emotional clouds are absent, take our bearings by the sun and by the stars of Beauty and of Truth, and then steer our course by those when the clouds have hidden them, knowing that these everlasting lights change not, although clouds may hide them and storm and darkness be around.

To understand, then, the law of periodicity, to base our ideals on the intellect and not only on the emotions (for the intellect stands by us when the emotions fail), these are two of our greatest means of becoming calm and peaceful in the midst of these changing moods. Then the steady attempt day by day to realise ourselves as the Eternal and the Changeless, and to put aside as not ourselves everything in us which is changing—that is the practice which leads us beyond the moods into peace. We must make it part of our daily thought. Let us give one minute, or a couple of minutes, in the morning, to this definite recognition: "I am the Changeless, the Eternal Self." Let us say it over, dwell upon it until it becomes a constant music in life, which we can hear at every moment when we turn our ears aside from the noise and tumult of the streets. Let us make it the habitual thought, and it will become in time the ruling thought, so that always there will be playing in us this idea: "I am the Changeless, the Eternal Self." The strength of that! The beauty of it! The glory of it! No one can even dream of it save those who for a moment have felt it. If we could always live in that, we

should be as Gods walking the earth: even glimpses
of it seem to bring the peace and the beauty of
Divinity into our petty and sordid lives.

And it is not so difficult a thing to think of this
each morning, and it is worth doing it. As we continually think, that we will become. All the Sages
have so taught. All the Scriptures of the world
proclaim it: as the man thinks so is he. And this
thought is of all the truest thought, the most absolutely true that can enter into the mind. We are
the Self, the living, the eternal, and the changeless.
That is the thought, then, that means peace, the
thought which makes all the moods unable to do
any real harm, to change our steps in life. That
they will not come, I do not say, but we shall not
blunder by identifying them with ourselves. We
shall no longer feel: "I am happy," "I am unhappy," "I am in light," "I am in darkness." We
shall say, when we feel that this lower sheath, this
lower mind, is the darkness or light, is happy or unhappy, is depressed or glad: "Let me see what I
can learn from that changing experience, what useful lesson for myself or for the helping of others
I can win from this experience through which the
lower part of me is passing." For that, after all,
is what we are here for, to learn what is to be learnt
through these lower principles, which are so changing, so volatile, so irrational, so foolish. We hold

them because they are valuable for the lessons that
they can pass on to us; and how should we ever
be able to help others, who are the victims of the
moods, unless we ourselves experienced those moods,
and experienced them when we were separate from
them? So long as we are their victims we cannot
help others, but if we did not feel them we should
not be able to help others any the more; for if we
did not feel them, we could not sympathise with
them and therefore could not help. And that also
I have noticed in the same eastern people I was
speaking of before. They often fail in sympathy,
because they do not experience the changes which
would make them able to understand and thereby
able to help. It is well that we should know by experience the pains which others suffer, but also
well that we should learn to know them so that we
can study them ourselves and not be conquered by
them. As long as we are conquered we cannot help
others. We have to learn at once to conquer and
also to help, to feel enough to sympathise but not
enough to blind. And suppose we could look at our
own moods from this standpoint we should find that
at once almost they had lost their power to sweep
us completely off our feet. We should find we were
becoming separate by the very fact of the analysis
we were carrying on; and although at first it seems
merely an intellectual exercise we should find it a

step towards realisation, we should feel ourselves apart in the very effort to imagine ourselves apart. Then we should reach that higher point so often spoken of in the *Bhagavad-Gîtâ*—to be above the pairs of opposites, above the guṇas, and also able to use them. For these are the great forces of the world which are affecting ourselves. These are the great energies of nature by which all is brought about that she brings about in her vast workings. While we are moved by them we are their slaves; when we begin to control them we can turn them to the noblest ends.

These moods of ours that seem so troublesome are really our best teachers, and as we learn that we shall value them rather than dislike them or shrink from them. We shall feel that they are only our enemies while they are unsubdued, according, again, to a great phrase which says: "To the unsubdued self, the Self verily becometh hostile as an enemy." The fact is that all these storms and whirlpools around us in the lower self are the very things that we have come into the world to live amongst in order that we may understand and use them; the things that we think are enemies are our best friends, they are the things that enable us to grow, that give us power to rule. The more we thus look on all in the clear light of the WISDOM, the more peaceful will our lives become; the more these moods are used

to understand others for the helping of them, the
more shall we rise above them as enemies until they
become our friends.   It is a great and a true saying: "We have never conquered our enemy until
we have turned him into our friend."   That is true
of the lower self, it is true of all the surging emotions, it is true of all the difficulties around us, of
all the trials and the ordeals through which we
pass.   We see them as serried hosts opposing our
onward path; We conquer them, and find that they
are great hosts behind us, ready to be led by us,
into the battle which shall win the victory of the
Self.

These are some of the lessons that I have learned
in the light and in the darkness, and far more in
the darkness than in the light.   So that I have
come to think that the times of light are only valuable as times of rest to prepare one for higher struggles and for greater conquests, and to look on the
darkness as the welcome time, the time in which
the Masters best are served, the time in which the
world is lifted a little higher towards the Light.
But it becomes true for us all at last that darkness
is as light and light as darkness; it becomes true
for us at last that darkness has no power to appeal
and no power to depress, that we know that those
who would bring the light must be those who live in
the dark, that the torch that sends its fire out

around itself is but a dark piece of wood, and in the
burning of the dark wood the light comes to others,
but not to itself. How shall we be able to go into the
darkness of all Christs who have saved the world,
except by learning to bear the passing darknesses
which creep over us from time to time? The greatest lesson of all that we have to learn, the lesson that
it is the one privilege of life to learn, and learn
perfectly, is the lesson that those who would help
the world must go below the world and lift it on
their shoulders, that those who would bring the
sunshine to others must accept the shadow and cloud
for themselves. But in the cloud there is a fire, and
in the fire there is the voice of the stillness, and
only those who have the courage to enter into the
cloud find therein the light which is the glory of
the Self; they see the Flame, they know themselves
as the bearers in the world of the Flame that illuminates, and they learn to know that the darkness
and the light are both alike, because they are equally
divine, because without the one the other could not
be.

Hypnotism I

Reprinted from "Lucifer," for October, 1889.

For many years the scientific world in Germany and France has been stirred to its depths by the experiments in hypnotism made by some of the leading physicians of each country. Both from the philosophical and the practical sides it has been realised that the strange power which formed the subject of investigation was one of supreme importance in its bearing on the constitution and conduct of man. Many of the records of alleged feats by witches and wizards of the Middle Ages—regarded by the nineteenth century as the mere drivel of superstitious ignorance—paled their ineffectual fires before the wonders of the new experimenters, while the visions of the saints received startling pendants from the Salpêtrière. In Germany, the State, with characteristic promptitude, appears to have armed itself against the practical dangers which threaten to assail society, with a law which forbids unqualified persons to practise hypnotism. On the other hand, the Materialists, recognising by a true intuition the

fatal character of the new departure for the Materialist philosophy, assailed the experimenters with
quite theological virulence, scoffing at their experiments and decrying their motives. The famous Dr.
Ludwig Büchner—whose services alike to medicine
and biology have been great—has vehemently at-
tacked those of his compatriots who have entered
the new path. In the last edition of his *Kraft und
Stoff* he speaks of "the legerdemain and claptrap of
magnetisers, clairvoyants, thaumaturgists, spiritualists, hypnotists and other jugglers."* Yet even he
alludes to the hypnotic as a "highly interesting condition"† and suggests that "it is probable that
hypnotism accounts for much that occurs at exhibi-
tions of animal magnetism." He remarks, indeed,
that "the whole effect is brought about by strictly
natural causes," a statement with which Theosophists, at least, will not quarrel.

Hypnotism—derived from ὕπνος, sleep—obtained
its name from its resemblance to somnambulism; in
most respects the hypnotic resembles the mesmeric or
magnetic trance, but differs from it in this, that
suggestions made to a person under hypnotism are
carried out when the hypnotic state has apparently
passed away, and not during the trance as in
ordinary mesmerism. Everyone has seen the mes-

* "Force and Matter," English translation, p. 338.
† Ibid, p. 346.

merised person obey the mesmeriser, accept his fic-
tions as facts, and perform at his bidding acts of the
most startling absurdity. But when the patient re-
covers his senses the spell is broken. Not so with
hypnotism. The patient opens his eyes, walks about,
goes away, performs the ordinary duties of life, but
obeys with undeviating regularity the impulse communicated by the hypnotiser, imagining all the time
that he is acting as a free agent while he is the bond-
slave of another's will. There can be little doubt.
however, that all these phenomena are but phases of
the same condition. Hypnotism is a new name, not
a new thing, its differentia being but extensions of
the old "mesmerism."

From the time of. Mesmer onwards attention has
from time to time been directed to the curious
phenomena obtained by mesmeric passes, fixity of
gaze, etc., but MM. Binet and Féré, in their work on
Le Magnétisme Animal,* give to Dr. James Braid, a
Manchester surgeon, the credit of being "the initiator
of the scientific study of animal magnetism" (p. 67).
"Magnetism and hypnotism," say these authors,
"are fundamentally synonymous terms, but the first
connotes a certain number of complex and extraordinary phenomena, which have always compro-
mised the cause of these fruitful studies. The term
hypnotism is exclusively applied to a definite nervous

* The references in the text are to be the English translation issued
under the title "Animal Magnetism."

state, observable under certain conditions, subject to general rules, produced by human and in no sense mysterious processes, and based on modifications of the functions of the patient's nervous system. Thus it appears that hypnotism has arisen from animal magnetism, just as the physico-medical sciences arose from the occult sciences of the Middle Ages." Braid found that many persons could hypnotise themselves by gazing fixedly at an object a little above the head in such a position that the eyes, when fixed on it squinted—or, to put the matter in a more dignified fashion, in such a position as induced a convergent and superior strabismus. The fixation of the attention was also necessary, and Braid considers that the insensibility of idiots to hypnotism arises from their incapacity for fixed attention (pp. 69, 70). At the Saltpêtrière, Dr. Charcot and his pupils, dealing with hysterical patients,* found that catalepsy could be produced by sudden sounds or vivid light, and that the patient could be made to pass from the cataleptic to the somnambulic or lucid hypnotic con- dition by friction on the scalp, pressure on the eye- balls, and other methods. Speaking generally, Dr. Richer states that stimulants "which produce a sud- den shock to the nervous system and cause a sleep whose abrupt commencement is accompanied by marked hysterical symptoms, such as twitching of

---

* Etudes cliniques sur la grande Hystérie. Par le Docteur Paul Richer.

the limbs, movements of swallowing, a little foam on the lips, pharyngeal murmur, etc., give rise to the nervous condition termed lethargy; while those which gently impress the nervous system and cause none of the hysterical symptoms to which I have alluded, produce a sleep which comes on progressively and without shock, the characteristics of which, differing from those of lethargy, belong to the special nervous state known under the name of somnambulic'' (p. 519), or hypnotic. The ticking of a watch, the steady gaze of the doctor, magnetic passes, a verbal command, etc., will throw many subjects into a hypnotic trance.

The condition of the hypnotised person may vary from insensibility to acute sensitiveness. The body may be rendered insensitive to pain, so that critical operations may be performed without the use of a material anæsthetic, and a number of such cases are on record. On the other hand hypnotisation often produces extreme hyperæsthesia. Binet and Fèrè say: ''In somnambulism [hypnotism] the senses are not merely awake, but quickened to an extraordinary degree. Subjects feel the cold produced by breathing from the mouth at a distance of several yards (Braid). Weber's compasses applied to the skin, produce a two-fold sensation with a deviation of $3°$, in regions where, during the waking state, it would be necessary to give the instrument a devia-

tion of 18° (Berger). The activity of the sense of
sight is sometimes so great that the range of sight
may be doubled, as well as sharpness of vision. The
sense of smell may be developed so that the subject is able to discover by its aid the fragments of a
visiting card which had been given him to smell
before it was torn up (Taguet). The hearing is so
acute that a conversation carried on on the floor below may be overheard (Azam). These are interesting but isolated facts. We are still without any col-
lective work on the subject, of which it would be
easy to make regular study, with the methods of investigation we have at our disposal. More careful
observations of the state of memory have been
made, but this state has only been studied as it has
been found during somnambulism, when it generally
displays the same hyper-excitability as the other
organs of the senses (Binet and Féreé, pp. 134, 135).

Memory may, indeed, be rendered extraordinarily
vivid under hypnotism. A poem read to a hypnotised person was repeated by her correctly; awake
she had forgotten it, but on again being hypnotised
she repeated it. A patient recalled the exact *menu*
of her dinner a week ago, though awake she could
only remember those of a day or two ago. Another
gave correctly and without hesitation the name of
a doctor whom she had seen in childhood, although
in her waking condition she, after some doubt, only

recalled the fact that he had been a physician in a children's hospital.

Many of the purely physical results are interesting in themselves, but, to the Theosophist, less suggestive than those which pass into the psychical realm. Contractures can be caused, and be transferred from one side to another, by a magnet. A limb can be rendered rigid, or can be paralyzed, and so on. An extremely curious experiment is the tracing of some words on the arm of a hypnotised subject with a blunt probe, the doctor then issued the following order: "This afternoon, at four o'clock, you will go to sleep, and blood will then issue from your arm, on the lines which I have now traced." The subject fell asleep at the hour named, the letters then appeared on his left arm, marked in relief, and of a bright red colour, which contrasted with the general paleness of the skin, and there were even minute drops of blood in several places. There was absolutely nothing to be seen on the right and paralyzed side [the patient was affected with hemiplegia and hemianæsthesia]. Mabille subsequently heard the same patient, in a spontaneous attack of hysteria, command his arm to bleed, and soon afterwards a cutaneous hæmorrhage just described was displayed. These strange phenomena recall, and also explain, the bleeding stigmata which have been repeatedly observed in the subjects of religious ecstasy, who have pictured to themselves the passion of Christ. Charcot and his pupils at the Salpêtrière have often produced the effects of burns upon the skin of hypnotised subjects by means of suggestion. The idea of the burn does not take effect immediately, but after the lapse of some hours (Binet and Féré, pp. 198, 199). The bearing of these experiments on the supposed miraculous impressions of the sacred stigmata is obvious, and offers one more of the many illustrations that the best way to eradicate superstition is not to deny the phenomena on which it rests, many of which are real, but to explain them, and to prove that they can be produced by natural means.

Muscular contractions of the limbs produce corresponding changes in the face, normally expressive of the feelings suggested by the artificially produced attitude. Richer states: ''A tragic attitude impresses sternness on the face, and the brows contract. On the other hand, if the two open hands are carried to the mouth, as in the act of blowing a kiss, a smile immediately appears on the lips. In this case the reaction of gesture on physiognomy is very remarkable and is produced with great exactitude. . . . One can thus infinitely vary the attitudes. Ecstasy, prayer, humility, sadness, defiance, anger, fear, can be represented. It is, indeed, startling to see how invariably a simple change in the position of the hands reacts on the features. If the open hand is stretched outwards, the facial expression is calm and benevolent, and changes to a smile if the arm is raised and the tips of the fingers brought to the mouth. But without altering the attitude of the arms, it suffices to close the subject's hands to see the benevolence give place to severity, which soon becomes anger if the clenching of the fist is increased. This phenomena may be unilateral. If the fist is clenched on one side and carried forward as in menace, the corresponding brow only is contracted. So if only one open hand is brought to the mouth, the smile will appear only on one side of the face. The two different attitudes may be simultaneously impressed on the two sides of the body, and each half of the face will reflect the corresponding expression'' (p. 669).

It is possible that these muscular contractions may give rise to no corresponding emotions, although it seems *primâ facie* probable that where the emotions constantly find expression in gestures the gestures should, in their turn, arouse the emotions. Yet it may be that the link is merely between muscle and muscle, and that the continual co-ordination results in a purely automatic action. We will, therefore, pass to phenomena in which the *psyche* is involved, and see what strange tricks can be played with it by the experimenter in hypnotism.

The lower senses of touch and taste and smell can be played with at will. A hypnotised patient, told that a bird had placed itself on her knee, stroked and caressed it (Richer, p. 645). "If a hallucinatory object, such as a lamp shade, is put into the subject's hands, and he is told to press it, he experiences a sensation of resistance and is unable to bring his hands together" (Binet and Féré, p. 213). Colocynth placed on the tongue is not tasted, odours are not smelt (Richer, p. 660). In the automatic state contact with familiar objects brings up the action constantly associated with them; given soap and water a patient will steadfastly wash her hands; given a match she will strike it, but is unconscious of pain if the flame touches her; given a probing pin, she will plunge it into her hand; given a book, she will begin to read it fluently and, when the book is turned upside down, continue to read it aloud in the reversed position (Richer, pp. 693-696). This automatic stage can be made to pass into the somnambulic, where the will is dominated, but where intelligence survives.

But it is when we come to the more intellectual sense of vision that we meet the most surprising phenomena. On a piece of white paper a white card was placed, and an imaginary line was drawn round this card, with a blunt pointer, without touching the paper, the patient being told that the line was being drawn. When she awake she was given the blank piece of paper, and she saw on it the rectangle which had *not* been traced; asked to fold the paper along the line she saw, she folded it exactly so that it was just covered by the card when the latter was placed on it (Richer, p. 723). A patient was told that she saw a black circle; on waking she looked about, rubbed her eyes, and on being questioned complained that she saw a black circle in whichever direction she turned her eyes, and that it was extremely annoying (*ibid*). A portrait was said to exist on a piece of blank cardboard; when the card was reversed the portrait was reversed with it, and it disappeared when the other side of the cardboard was shown, although the changes of position were made out of sight of the patient (Binet and Féré, p. 224). Such a portrait is visible to the patient through an opera glass, and is magnified or diminished like a real object. Again, a patient, Bar——, was told that Dr. Charcot was present, and although he was not there she addressed him, told to listen to the music she heard an imaginary concert; told that a number of children were present, she made the gestures of taking them in her arms and kissing them, described the colour of their hair and eyes; while another patient complained that their play irritated her, and that the noise they made was intolerable.

More complex visions can be made to pass before the eyes; suggest to a patient that Paradise lies open before her, and she will see angels, and saints, the Virgin, and so on, the details of the vision varying with the richness of imagination of the patient. Sometimes it is the devil whose presence is suggested, and the most vivid fear and anger are expressed. Surely we have here the key to the visions of ecstatic nuns; the fixed gaze at the crucifix with upturned eyes is the very position for self-hypnotisation; the matter of the visions is suggested by the pressure of the dominant idea; while the certitude of the patients as to the reality of the visions would be complete.

Yet more curious are the phenomena connected with the rendering of an object or a person invisible by suggestion. Ten similar cards were shown to a hypnotised subject, and she was told that she could not see one of them. When she was awakened that card remained invisible; and similar results were obtained with keys, thermometers, and other objects (Richer, p. 729). To another was said "You will not see M. X.," and on waking M. X. was invisible to her. We once suggested to a hypnotic subject that she would cease to see F—— but would continue to hear his voice. On waking the subject heard the voice of an invisible person, and looked about the room to discover the cause of this singular phenomenon, asking us about it with some uneasiness. We said, jestingly, "F—— is dead, and it is his ghost which speaks to you." The subject is intelligent, and in her normal state she would probably have taken the jest at its true value; but she was dominated by the suggestion of anæsthesia, and readily adopted the explanation. When F—— spoke again he said that he had died the night before, and that his body had been taken to the post-mortem room. The subject clasped her hands with a sad expression, and asked when he was to be buried, as she wished to be present at the religious service. "Poor young man!" she said; "he was not a bad man." F——, wishing to see how far her credulity would go, uttered groans and complained of the autopsy of his body which was going on. The scene then became tragic, for the emotion of the subject caused her to fall backwards in an incipient attack of hysteria, which we promptly arrested." (Binet and Féré, pp. 312, 313). The most suggestive experiment was one in which F—— was rendered invisible; the subject was then awakened, and on enquiring for F—— was told that he had left the room. She was then told that she might retire, and went towards the door against which F—— had placed himself. Unable to see him she came in contact with him, and on a second experiment to reach the door, became alarmed at the incomprehensible resistence and refused to again go near it. A hat was placed on his head, and "words cannot express" the subject's surprise, since it appeared to her that the hat was suspended in the air. Her surprise was at its height when F—— took off the hat and saluted her with it several times; she saw the hat, without any support, describing curves in the air. F—— then put on a cloak, and she saw the cloak moving and assuming the form of a person. "It is," she cried, "like a hollow puppet." A number of other experiments were tried with her, leaving no doubt that she was completely unconscious of F——'s presence (Binet and Féré, pp. 306-308).

In another class of experiments the subject's personality was changed. On one occasion we told X—— that she had become M. F——, and after some resistance she accepted the suggestion. On awaking she was unable to see M. F——, who was present; she imitated his manner, and made the gesture of putting both her hands in the pockets of an imaginary hospital apron. From time to time she put her hand to her lip as if to smooth her moustache, and looked about her with assurance. But she said nothing. We asked her whether she was acquainted with X——. She hesitated for a moment, and then replied, with a contemptuous shrug of the shoulders: "Oh yes, a hysterical patient. What do you think of her? She is not too

wise'' (ibid. pp. 215, 216). Another patient person-
ated in succession a peasant woman, an actress, a
general, an archbishop, a nun, speaking appropri-
ately in each character (Richer, pp. 729, 730).

There is another class of phenomena which opens
up serious dangers of a practical nature. A suggestion made to a hypnotised subject may be carried
out when the subject is awake, either immediately,
or days or months afterwards, and this obedience is
blind to consequences and to every consideration of
right or wrong. We have a personality, not a machine, but a personality which is the puppet of another's will. Dr. Richer remarks: ''In the latter
state (cataleptic) the subject is an automaton, without conscience or spontaniety, only moving under
the impulse of sensorial stimuli coming from without. The stimulus alone matters, and not the person who supplies it. The personality of the operator
is indifferent. All the responses are of the nature of
reflex actions, without any participation of the intellectual activity other than such as may be necessary for the production. The somnambulist, on the
other hand, is no longer a simple machine. He is the
slave of the will of another, the veritable *subject* of
the operator. His automatism consists in servitude
and obedience. But certain consciousness exists
other than that of the waking state. A new personality is created, which may give rise to those strange

phenomena described under the name of duplication
of consciousness or of personality. There is really
a somnambulic Ego, while there is no cataleptic
Ego'' (p. 789).

It is in this somnambulic stage that occur the
phenomena now to be considered. A hypnotised subject is required to steal some object; sometimes she
resists, but insistance generally overcomes this resistance; only in a few cases has it been found impossible to conquer it. On waking, the patient
watches her opportunity and performs the theft.
And here comes in the curious fact, that the subject
shows cunning and intelligence in carrying out the
suggestion. One patient, told to steal the handkerchief of a certain person, presently feigned dizziness,
and staggering against the person stole the handkerchief. In another case, the subject suddenly
asked the owner of the handkerchief what he had
in his hand, and stole it as he, in surprise, looked
at his hand. Another, told to poison X—— with a
glass of water, offered, it with the remark that it
was a hot day. ''If Z—— is armed with a paper-
knife and ordered to kill X—— she says, ''Why
should I do it? He has done me no harm.'' But if
the experimenter insists, the slight scruple may be
overcome, and she soon says: ''If it must be done
I will do it.'' On awaking she regards X—— with
a perfidious smile, looks about her, and suddenly

strikes him with the supposed dagger. The patient will find reasons to excuse her act; one who had struck a man with a pasteboard knife under suggestion was asked why she killed him. She looked at him fixedly for a moment and then replied with an expression of ferocity, "He was an old villain, and wished to insult me" (Binet and Féré, pp. 286-291).

Without further accumulating these phenomena let us consider whether any, and if any, what explanation is possible.

And first from the standpoint of Materialism. It is possible to explain on a materialistic hypothesis the muscular contractions and co-ordinations, and the automatic actions succeeding contact with familiar articles. But even in the automatic stage, explanation is lacking of the fluent reading of a reversed book by an uneducated person. It is, however, in the phenomena of memory, of vision of the non-existent, of inhibited vision, that materialistic explanation seems to me to be impossible.

Memory is the faculty which receives the impress of our experiences, and preserves them; many of these impressions fade, and we say we have forgotten. Yet it is clear that these impressions may be revived. They are, therefore, not destroyed, but they are so faint that they sink below the threshold of consciousness, and so no longer form part of its normal content. If thought be but a "mode of motion," memory must be similarly regarded; but it is not possible to conceive that each impression of our past life, recorded in consciousness, is still vibrating in some group of brain cells, only so feeble that it does not rise above the threshold. For these same cells are continually being thrown into new groupings for new vibrations, and these cannot all co-exist, and the fainter ones be capable of receiving fresh impulse which may so intensify their motion as to again raise them into consciousness. Now if these vibrations—memory, if we have only matter in motion, we know the law of dynamics sufficiently well to say that if a body be set vibrating, and new forces be successively brought to act upon it and set up new vibrations, there will not be in that body the co-existence of each separate set of vibrations successively impressed upon it, but it will vibrate in a way differing from each single set, and compounded of all. So that memory, as a mode of motion, would not give us a record of the past, but would present us with a new story, the resultant of all those past vibrations, and this would be ever changing, as fresh impressions, causing new vibrations, came in to modify the resultant of the old. On the other hand, let us suppose a conscious Ego, retaining knowledge of all its past experiences, but only able to impress such of them on the organ of consciousness as the laws of the material organism permit, the threshold of consciousness dividing what it can thus impress from what it cannot; that threshold would vary with the material conditions of the moment, rising and falling with the state of the organism, and what we call memory would be the content of the material consciousness, bounded by the threshold at any given instant. Now, under hypnotisation an extraordinary revival of the past occurs, and impressions long since faded come out clear-cut on the tablet of memory. Is it not a possible hypothesis that the process of hypnotisation causes a shifting of the threshold of consciousness, and so brings into sight what is always there but what is normally concealed? The existence of the Ego is posited by Theosophy, and it seems to me that the phenomena of hypnotisation require it.

How can the Materialist explain the vision of non-existent things? We know what are the mechanical conditions of vision in the animal body; the rays reflected from the object, the blows of the ethereal waves on the retina, the vibrating nerve-cells, the optic centre; the perception belongs to the world of mind. But in seeing the invisible we have the perception, but with none of the steps that normally lead up to it; the suggestion of the hypnotiser awakens the perception, and the mind creates its own object of sense to respond to it. Again, it must be the perceptive power, not the sense-channel, which is paralysed when objects and persons become invisible. Take the case of F—— and his cloak; certain rays from the body of F—— struck the retina of the patient, but no perception followed; for the cloak to be seen normally, rays from it must traverse exactly the same line as those from his body, impinge on the same retinal cells, throw into vibration the same nervous cord, and so be perceived. If the inhibition were of the nerve elements, the rays from the cloak would be stopped like those from the body round which it was wrapped. The inhibition was not of nerve, but of mind; the operator had entered the subject world of the patient and had laid his hand on the faculty, not on the instrument. If perception be only the result of vibrating cells, how comes it then that cells may vibrate and the result be absent? that in two cases the vibration may be equally set up, the same cells be in motion, and yet that perception follows the one vibration and not the other? A still further complication arises when the cloak is seen, though the body is interposed between it and the organ of vision. If perception result from cell-vibration, how can perception arise when no cell-vibration is set up?

But it seems that it is not only the perceptive faculty that the operator may bring under his control: he may lay hold of the will and compel the patient to acts, and so become the master of his personality. A terrible power, yet one that can no longer be regarded as doubtful, and which recalls the old-world stories of "possession," throwing on them a new and lurid light. How many of the tales of magic powers, which changed people's characters and drove them in obedience to the will of the "magician," are now explicable as hypnotic effects? How often may the "evil eye" have caused injury, by deliberate suggestion as Charcot thus caused a burn? I have often thought that there must have been a basis of fact underlying the widespread belief in witchcraft; and the possession of hypnotising power, aided by the exaggerations of fear and credulity, would amply suffice to account for it. The general belief in evil spirits would lead to the ascription of the results to their agency, and the very ignorance of the nature of their own power by the "magicians" would foster the notion of supernatural interference.

The study of hypnotism drives us, if we would remain within the realm of natural law, of causation, into the belief that the mind is not the mere outcome of physical motion, however closely the two may be here normally related. That while the brain is "the organ of mind" on this plane, it is literally the organ and not the mind; and that it is possible, so to speak, to get behind the organ and seize upon the mind itself, dethroning the individu-

ality and assuming usurped control. On this hypothesis the results of the experiments become intelligible, and we can dimly trace the *modus operandi*.

Theosophists may well utilise this new departure
in science to gain a hearing for their own luminous
philosophy, for the Western World cannot turn a
deaf ear to the testimony of its own experts, and
the experiments of those very experts force on the
mind the impossibility of the mind and the will being the mere result of molecular vibration. Once
carry a thoughtful Materialist so far, and he will be
bound to go farther, and thus the very triumph
of Materialistic science shall lead to the downfall of
its philosophy.

Hypnotism II

Reprinted from "The Universal Review" for February, 1890.

I.—THE HISTORY.

The attention of the scientific world in France and in Germany has long been directed to the curious phenomena which are classed as "hypnotic" and for years past experiments of the most searching character have been carried on by experts, notably at the Salpêtrière and in Nancy. In Germany, Heidenhain, one of the most eminent of German physiologists, has, since 1880, been investigating these phenomena, attracted thereto by the experiments of Carl Hansen, a Dane, the gentleman who in October last founded a Hypnotic Society in London, for the systematic study and use of Hypnotism. The phenomena are interesting, not only as being curious in themselves, and as promising to place in the hands of the physician a useful therapeutic agent, but also for the light they throw on the physical constitution of man, and on those subtle problems of life and mind which occupy the attention of the acutest thinkers of our time.

There can be no doubt, in the light of our present knowledge that many of the "miraculous" cures credited to prophet and saint were the results of magnetic power; that the ecstasy of the saint is reproduced in the hypnotic trance; that witches and wizards may be rivalled by the mesmeriser. Much that was obscure is now illuminated, and the Salpêtrière patient explains the sybil and the seeress. We see prophecies, visions, possessions, the evil eye, magic control, all reproduced under conditions which render possible careful scrutiny and deliberate investigation.

The scope of Hypnotism will, however, be poorly understood if we confine ourselves to the rigid experimentation of the French doctors. Valuable as is their work, placing Hypnotism among the experimental sciences on a basis that none can challenge, we shall only understand its bearing by studying it from a standpoint that renders visible a wider horizon, and enables us to see it in relation to its historical evolution, as well as in its most modern presentment.

The soothing and curative power that lies in the human touch was long known ere the resemblance of some of its properties to those of the magnet gave rise to the name of Animal Magnetism. Solon (B.C. 637-558) speaks of the fury of disease being soothed by the gentle stroking of the hand,* and in China the origin of the practice of curing diseases by the laying on of hands is lost in antiquity. Celsus records the fact that Asclepiades, the Greek "father of physic," "practised light friction as a means of inducing sleep in phrensy and insanity; and, what is more remarkable, he says that by too much friction there was a danger of inducing lethargy."† The Chaldean priests, the Pharisees, the Hindus, and other civilised people of antiquity, also practised cure by touch. There can be little doubt that this custom is alluded to in 2 Kings v. 11, where Naaman is represented as saying that he thought the Jewish prophet would "strike his hand over the place and recover the leper." The Egyptian sculptures show figures in magnetic positions, and the habit of taking to the sick cloths impregnated with the magnetism of a holy person is often met with in antiquity, and is spoken of in Acts xix. 12. The cures wrought by Vespasian at Alexandria, as recorded by Suetonius and Tacitus, were obviously magnetic, and the idea of the curative properties of the "king's touch" was but an inheritance from the time when the priestly functions attached to the royal office carried with them this healing power.

Nor was this use of human magnetism for the cure

---

* "Apud Stobæum." Translated in Stanley's "History of Philosophy," 1666.

† "Somnolism and Psychism." By J. W. Haddock, M.D., 1851, p. 7.

of diseases the only kind of magnetic phenomenon known to the ancients. Hippocrates, Aristotle, Galen, and other classical authors mention somnambulism, a state which may supervene naturally or be artificially induced, and is, in either case, a phenomenon now included under "hypnotism." Nor can there be much doubt as to the nature of the utterances of the sacred virgins in Pagan temples. Of these Dr. Haddock says:

From what is known of the practices, the long vigils and fastings, and the peculiar attitudes and manners of the Sybils, there can be little doubt that by various means, kept secret from the multitude, a condition similar, if not identical with the higher mesmeric, or *psychic* state, as it is proposed to call it, was induced; and that the Sybils and utterers of oracles were, at times, really clairvoyant and in a state of trance. Saint Justin said "that the Sybils spoke many great things with justice and with truth, and *that when the instinct which animated them ceased to exist, they lost the recollection of all they had declared.*" It will be seen in the sequel that this is so strikingly in accordance with mesmeric sleep or trance, as to leave scarcely a doubt of its identity with it.*

It is not definitely known when the properties of magnetised iron and steel were first discovered, the Chinese claiming to be the first to use the compass, but it is certain that the use of the magnet for curative purposes can point to a respectable antiquity. Paracelsus (A.D. 1493-1541) seems to have been the first, among Westerns at least, to ascribe magnetism to the human body, and to suggest the use of this

* Ibid, pp. 6, 7.

human magnetism for the cure of disease; in his time magnets must have been used for this purpose, as we can judge not only from his expression of "human magnetism," but also from a work by Cardan, dated 1584 in which "there is an account of an experiment in anæsthesia, produced by the magnet," and it is stated that " it was then customary to magnetise rings, which were worn round the neck or the arm, in order to cure nervous diseases."*

Pomponatius (A.D. 1462-1525) had already pointed to the fact, which he speaks of as generally acknowledged, that some persons are "gifted with the faculty of curing certain diseases, in virtue of an emanation from themselves which by the power of the will and the imagination they are able to direct to the sick."† "When those who are endowed with this faculty," says Pomponatius, "operate by employing the force of the imagination and the will, this force affects their blood and their spirits, which produce the intended effects, by means of an evaporation thrown outwards."‡ He considers that health may be communicated to a sick person, as disease may be communicated to a healthy one; and he alleges that matter, the elements themselves, can be made subject to man by this magnetic force. In 1621 the

+ "Animal Magnetism." By Binet and Féré. English Translation, 1888, p. 2.
† "Human Magnetism." By W. Newnham, 1845, pp. 149, 150.
‡ Quoted in "Isis Revelata," by J. C. Colquhoun, 1836, vol. i., p. 152.

celebrated Van Helmont (A.D. 1577-1644) published in Paris a remarkable work on "The Magnetic Cure of Wounds," in which he defended magnetism as a curative as against a Jesuit, Father Robert, who had maintained that certain cures were the work of the devil. "Magnetism," he writes, "is a universal agent; there is nothing in it but the name; and it is a paradox only to those who are disposed to ridicule everything, and who ascribe to the influence of Satan all those phenomena which they cannot explain." He defines magnetism as "that occult influence which bodies exert over each other at a distance, whether by attraction or by repulsion," and considers that it acts through a fluid, the *Magnale Magnum,* an ethereal spirit which penetrates all bodies, and in the human frame is found in the blood, and is directed by the will. Man can so use it as to affect objects at a distance, and the strength of his impulsion depends on the energy and concentration of his volition. "This magical power lies dormant in man." So thoroughly convinced was Van Helmont of the reality of the magnetic force, that when the plague was raging at Brussels, he went thither to tend the sick.* Many other authors wrote on the same lines during the seventeenth century, as Sir Kenelm Digby, in 1660, William Maxwell, 1679, and Robert Fludd. A most remarkable quotation from a

* See "Isis Revelata," vol. i., pp. 154-161.

work published in 1673 by. Sebastian Wirdig, is given by Mr. Colquhoun: "Totus mundus constat et positus est in magnetismo; omnes sublunarium vicissitudines fiunt per magnetismum; vita conservatur magnetismo; interitus omnium reruni fiunt per magnetismum."† In 1889, Dr. Buck writes, in words that are wellnigh an echo of the seventeenth century philosopher: "We thus discern an underlying substance everywhere diffused, of great tenuity, permeating all things as the common basis of matter and force. This substance, with its characteristic polarizing tendency, and its universal diffusibility, outwardly displayed in atoms of elements, and in all objective phenomenal nature, is magnetism."*

One of the most remarkable of the practical magnetisers of the seventeenth century was an Irish gentleman, named Valentine Greatrakes, who published an autobiographical sketch in 1666. Among his patients were the philosopher Cudworth and the astronomer Flamsteed, while Robert Boyle President of the Royal Society, bears witness to the reality of his cures. Dr. George Rust, Bishop of Derry, writes as follows on what he himself saw, and his testimony is confirmed by members of the Royal Society, physicians, and others, who carefully examined into the alleged facts:

I was three weeks together with him at my Lord Conway's,

† Ibid, p. 150.
* "A Study of Man." By J. D. Buck, M.D., 1889, p. 31.

and saw him, I think, lay his hands upon a thousand persons;
and really there is something in it more than ordinary; but I
am convinced it is not miraculous. I have seen pains strangely
fly before his hands, till he hath chased them out of the body—
dimness cleared and deafness cured by his touch; twenty persons, at several times, in fits of the falling sickness, were in
two or three minutes brought to themselves, so as to tell where
their pain was; and then he hath pursued it till he hath drawn
it out at some extreme part; running sores of the king's evil
dried up, and kernels brought to a suppuration by his hand;
grievous sores of many months' date in a few days healed;
obstructions and stoppings removed; cancerous knots in the
breast dissolved, etc.

The Bishop says further that the cures often took
some time, and that patients often relapsed, while
with others he could do nothing. His method was
placing his hand on the affected part, and stroking
lightly from above downwards. The Royal Society
considered that there was "a sanative influence in
Mr. Greatrakes' body," and in a book which contains an article on the cures by Robert Boyle, is a
remarkable cure of leprosy by "stroaking" by Greatrakes.*

In the eighteenth century John Joseph Gassner
(born 1727) performed a number of cures, chiefly
among patients suffering from epilepsy and other
nervous complaints; a full account may be read in
the German *Archiv für den Thierischen Magnetis-
mus*, published at Leipzig.

From this rough sketch it will be seen that when

* "Isis Revelata," vol. i., pp. 203 to 207. See also Newnham's
"Human Magnetism," pp. 150, 151, and "Somnolism and Psychism,"
pp. 8,9.

the man was born who was destined to give his name to this little-understood natural force, its existence had long been known, and it had been largely utilised. Anthony Mesmer (1734-1815) was born, some say at Weiler, in Germany, some at Mersburg, in Switzerland, and while still young went to Vienna to study medicine. He did not take his doctor's degree until 1766, when he chose for his subject "The Influence of the Planets on the Human Body," following Paracelsus in the theory that the planets influenced the human body through a subtle magnetic fluid. A Jesuit professor of astronomy at Vienna, named Hehl, drew his attention to the loadstone as a curative agent, and Mesmer and Hehl together performed a number of experiments with magnetised steel plates. Some jealousy arose between them, apparently from Mesmer having discovered that "magnetic passes," movements of the hand from above downwards, much increased the value of the steel plates; what is certain is that Mesmer and Hehl fell out, and that Mesmer's proceedings so aroused against him the medical faculty of Vienna that he was obliged to leave that city. He visited various towns, performing many cures in the hospitals and elsewhere, and after a varied experience came to the conclusion that the human body could produce effects similar to those produced by the magnet, and that "animal magnetism" was a powerful curative agent.

About this time a man named Perkins in England, patented for the cure of disease some "metallic tractors," which appear to have resembled the steel plates of Mesmer and Hehl; Perkins, however, did not grasp the luminous idea of Mesmer, that the curative power lay in the human body, and his discovery was discredited when Drs. Haygarth and Falconer produced with wooden tractors results similar to those produced by his metallic ones.* Mesmer, who had hold of the right principle, proceeded with his cures, and in 1778 arrived in Paris, whither his fame had preceded him. He published in 1779 a pamphlet, in which he laid down his theory of animal magnetism, claiming that his "system would furnish fresh knowledge of the nature of fire and light, as well as of the theory of attraction, of flux and reflux, of the magnet and electricity." "This principle can cure nervous diseases directly and others indirectly. By its aid the physician is enlightened as to the use of drugs; he perfects their action, provokes and directs at his will salutary crises, so as to completely master them." He summarised his theory in twenty-seven propositions, many of which are recognised as true to-day, however startling they may have appeared to be to the science of the eighteenth century. The human body, he alleged, showed polarity—a fruitful idea, des-

* "Somnolism and Psychism," pp. 9, 10.

tined to have great results—and animal magnetism could be communicated to living and non-living agents, and operate from afar. Mesmer's first convert was Dr. D'Eslon, but doctors for the most part were bitterly hostile, and the Medical Faculty of Paris suspended Dr. D'Eslon and denounced Mesmer and all his works, finally, in 1784, prohibiting the practice of animal magnetism by doctors under penalty of expulsion.

Despite this official excommunication, Mesmer had the bad taste to continue performing cures, and Paris, palpitating with new ideas, intoxicated with new liberty, went well-nigh mad over him. Fashionable society thronged his consulting-room and fought for admission at his doors. Unfortunately Mesmer was not strong enough to master his own popularity, and lent himself to follies which brought discredit on his really great powers. Clad in purple silk he wandered through the crowd of patients, amid soft music, in carefully subdued light, touching one with a metallic rod, another with the hand, provoking and controlling passionate excitement. The patients were seated round a *baquet,* or trough, the contents of which set up a magnetic current; they were mostly dilettante, hysterical, credulous men and women of the court, in search of some new excitement. What wonder that with such a crowd, dominated by the handsome presence and undoubtedly strong magnetic powers of the marvellous doctor, with the expectation of the wonderful ensuring its own realisation, with the hysterical contagion to which a crowd is always liable, what wonder that convulsive cries were provoked, and scandalous scenes enacted?

Outside Paris, numerous "Harmonic Societies" were established, the members of which magnetised the sick poor gratuitously and communicated to each other the noteworthy facts which occurred within their experience.* At last it was felt that is was necessary to institute a careful inquiry into the whole subject, and Louis XVI., in 1784, issued a mandate to the Medical Faculty in Paris, desiring them to appoint commissioners and draw up a report. Two Commissions were appointed, one of members of the Academy of Sciences, including such men as Franklin, Bailly, Lavoisier, and Guillotin; the other members of the Society of Physicians, among whom De Jussieu was the most famous. These Commissions reported against Mesmer, considering that his cures were due to imagination of the patients, and that his system was injurious to morality. Attention was drawn in a special report to the de-

* See "Isis Revelata," vol. i., pp. 238, 239. In this learned work is given a very full account of Mesmer, and the reader who desires to investigate the whole question of Animal Magnetism can find no more useful treatise, as it is crowded with references to the literature of the subject in ancient and modern times.

tails of the system. "The magnetiser generally keeps the patient's knees enclosed within his own," "the hand is laid on the hypochondriac region" and other sensitive parts of the body, and thus crises were provoked of a hysterical nature, detrimental to moral dignity and self-control. "Imagination, imitation, touches, such are the real causes of the effects attributed to animal magnetism. The methods of magnetism being dangerous, it follows that all public treatment in which magnetic practices are used must in the long run, have the most lamentable results." But among these eminent men one of the most eminent dissented from the report presented by his Commission, and, while combating the theory of magnetism, refused to refer to imagination all the strange phenomena he had watched with the trained observation of the naturalist. Of this dissident, De Jussieu, Dr. Paul Richer says:

A faithful and accurate observer, he had noted facts that had escaped the attention of the commissioners, or that they had voluntarily neglected. These facts are not beyond criticism, and moreover they are insufficient as the foundation of a theory, be it what it may. But it is not the less true that De Jussieu is the one *savant* who suspected that among all the phenomena, more or less strange and incoherent, then put to the debit and credit of animal magnetism, there were some in which the unknown was lying hidden, worthy of profound examination, and meriting something better than disdain or a simple non-acceptance.*

* "La Nouvelle Revue," August, 1882. "Magnétisme Animal et Hypnotisme." Par Paul Richer.

The insight of De Jussieu was to be justified by the future. It may be noted also that Cuvier (1769 to 1832), who was in 1800 appointed Professor of Natural Philosophy in the College de France, later endorsed De Jussieu rather than his colleagues. In the second volume of his *Anatomie Comparée*, he writes:

I must confess that it is very difficult to distinguish the effect of the imagination of the patient from the physical effect produced by the operator. The effects, however, which are produced upon persons already insensible before the commencement of the operation, those which take place in others after the operation has deprived them of sensibility, and those which are manifested by animals, do not permit us to doubt that the proximity of two animated bodies, in certain positions and with certain motions, has a real effect, independently of all participation of the imagination of one of them. It seems sufficiently evident, too, that these effects are owing to some sort of communication which is established between their nervous systems.*

The belief in Animal Magnetism, which was now spoken of as Mesmerism, was not, however, to be crushed out by the unfavourable reports of the Commissions. As Mr. Colquhoun well says, the facts "almost daily disclosed were much too numerous, too unambiguous, and too firmly established, to be overthrown even by the united force of learning, prejudice, ingenuity, ridicule, invective, and perse cution." In Germany, Lavater, in 1787, drew to it the attention of the medical world, and it has since

* Quoted in "Isis Revelata," vol. i., p. 74.

steadily flourished there, and has given birth to a widespread scientific literature. In France, despite the Revolution, its study proceeded, although Mesmer left the country,* and three distinct schools of magnetism were established: that of Mesmer, proceeding by touches, friction and pressure, the use of the *baquet,* of magnetised water and plates applied to the stomach; a treatment provocative of violent convulsions and crises; that of Barbarin, which disregarded physical means and relied on the will of the operator; and the most celebrated of all, that of the Marquis Chastenet de Puységur, a pupil of Mesmer, who took for his motto ''Croyez et veuillez,'' and used magnetic passes without contact. De Puységur practised chiefly on the peasants of his vicinity, and worked a large number of cures, full accounts of which may be read in his published works.† It is to De Puységur that we owe the first description of the magic trance, or lucid somnambulism, a discovery since so fruitful in results. A young peasant, named Victor, was suffering from an affection of the chest, and was magnetised by De Puységur, who thus describes the case:

What was my surprise to see, in seven minutes, this man

* Mesmer died in 1815, at Mersburg, on the Lake of Constance, deeply beloved of the poor, to whose treatment he consecrated his powers in his later years.

† In the third edition, 1820, of his ''Mémoires pour servir a l'histoire et à l'etablissement du Magnétisme Animal,'' I find no less than eight works advertised as from his pen. The ''Mémoires'' has for stamp a heartsease, surrounded by rays and ringed with the words, ''Thought moves matter.''

fall into a tranquil sleep in my arms, without convulsions or pains. I hastened the crisis, a proceeding that caused some giddiness; he spoke aloud on matters of būsiness. When it seemed to me that his thoughts must affect him unpleasantly, I stopped them, and sought to inspire merrier ones; this did not require much effort, and he became quite content, fancying that he was drawing for a prize, dancing at a fête, etc. . . . I encouraged these ideas in him, and thus obliged him to move actively in his chair, as though dancing to a tune which, by singing it *mentally*, I made him repeat out loud.*

De Puységur tells us of a peasant "the most stupid man in the countryside," who taught him methods of magnetising when in the "clairvoyant" state, and relates how his patient, in the magnetic state, "was no longer stupid, scarce able to stumble through a sentence, but becomes a being I can hardly describe, to whom I need not speak, for he understands me and answers me if I merely think in his presence."† This lucid somnambulic state, as it has since been termed, attracted general attention, and the popularity of De Puységur rivalled that of Mesmer.

Gradually doctor after doctor in France experimented in Animal Magnetism, or Mesmerism, with varying results. In 1820, in consequence of the investigations of a young medical man, Dr. A. Bertrand, the hospitals were opened for experiments, and the student may read Baron Du Potet's large collec-

* "Mémoires," pp. 21, 22.

† Ibid, pp. 27-29. The student will find a large number of in-structive cases in this work.

tion of his personal experiences. He relates some remarkable cures wrought by himself; but the "unreliability" of the little-understood natural agent in different hands and the prejudice of the medical profession, barred the way to its general adoption.* Experiments successfully performed by one person on one day, failed at the hands of another person on the next day, and, the conditions of success not yet being understood, the failure seemed inexplicable and discouragement supervened. It was forgotten that, in the investigation of every newly-discovered natural force, similar successes and failures occurred; and it was as rash to denounce Animal Magnetism as unreliable because beginners blundered, as to deny that electricity could be produced by friction because a machine working in a moisture-laden atmosphere threw off no sparks.

In 1825, however, Animal Magnetism had progressed so much that it again applied in Paris for scientific *imprimatur*, and after five years of patient investigation a Commission, named by the Academy of Medicine, reported strongly in favour, and declared that "the Academy should encourage research into Animal Magnetism, as a very curious branch of psychology and natural history."† But the reading of this report, presented by M. Husson, raised a

* "Manuel de l'Etudiant Magnétiseur." Par Baron Du Potet. Quatrième édition, Paris, 1868.

† "Nouvelle Revue" *loc. cit.* p. 593.

storm; one doctor declared that the Academy was being entertained with miracles and another, that if the alleged facts were true they would destroy half our physiological knowledge; so that, finally, the report was shelved. In 1837, another Commission, composed almost entirely of the opponents of magnetism, was appointed, and another report issued, this time, as was expected, in hostility; this report was adopted by the Academy, and was clinched by the offer of a prize of 3,000 francs by M. Burdin, to anyone who could read without using the eyes and in darkness. M. Pigeaire, a doctor of Montpelier, submitted his daughter, who was able to read with her eyes bandaged, when in the magnetic trance; a commission was thereupon appointed to examine this child, who had her eyes covered with cotton-wool, and then carefully bandaged; the judges appear to have been harsh, and to have distressed the sensitive, who was accustomed to use the tips of her fingers for reading, as do many somnambulists, and after much discussion the prize remained unrewarded. M. Pigeaire then offered a prize of 30,000 francs to anyone, not in the magnetic trance, who could read, wearing his daughter's bandage, and this prize also remained unwon. It may be remarked that the tips of the fingers, the pit of the stomach, and the centre of the crown of the head, are used by somnambulists for reading;

a book placed in contact with one of these parts of the body is fluently read.

So far as France was concerned, Animal Magnetism now remained under a cloud, but in England it made great progress. Dr. Abercrombie, Dr. Haddock, Dr. Elliott, and many others, investigated it, and in most cases practised it, and with remarkable success. But the founder of the modern school of "hypnotism" was Dr. Braid, a Manchester surgeon, who seeing some experiments performed by Lafontaine, a Swiss mesmerist, in 1841, and believing him to be fraudulent, set himself to work to discover the supposed imposition. He, however, came to the conclusion that the incapacity of the mesmerised patient to open his eyes was a real incapacity, and he began to experiment upon his friends, with the view of producing a similar phenomenon. He found that this closing of the eyes could be brought about by a fixed gaze at an object placed slightly above the eyes, so that a convergent strabismus was induced. When the hypnotic state was thus obtained, he found that the patient could be readily influenced, and that, by placing him in given attitudes, the emotions normally expressed by these attitudes could be produced in him at will. He further discovered that the senses often become abnormally acute under hypnotism, and that hallucinations could be imposed on the subject by "suggestion," *i.e.*, that a direction to see something on awaking was followed by a hallucination when the subject came out of the trance condition. Since the time of Braid, the whole question has been studied in the most strictly scientific spirit, experiments have been performed under rigid test conditions, and hypnotism is no longer an alien in the scientific world, but an accepted denizen, well worthy of careful attention. The world-famous experiments of Charcot and his colleagues at the Salpêtrière, and those of Liébault at Nancy, have for ever rendered impossible the recurrence of the follies of 1784 and 1837. The revival of the study in France was due to the experiments of Azam, a Bordeaux surgeon, in 1850, and various works on it appeared up to the year 1866, when Liébault published the results of his investigations. In 1878, the Salpêtrière school first attracted public notice, and from that time forward scepticism has been replaced by study in the scientific world.

In the Salpêtrière every source of modern science has been utilised to shut out the possibility of fraud, and those who doubt the results startled by their amazing character, will do well to study Dr. Paul Richer's monumental work, *Etudes Cliniques sur la Grande Hystérie, ou Hystero-Epilepsie*. It has been found by numerous experiments that the tracings obtained by attaching a tambour to the arm and a pneumatograph to the chest of a subject thrown into

the cataleptic state are wholly different from those
obtained from a subject in the normal condition; for
instance, while a strong man may simulate some
forced position, and the eye of the observer may be
unable to distinguish any difference between his attitude and that of a cataleptic patient placed in a
similar attitude, yet the strain in his case will be
made evident by the tracings obtained from him,
which are wholly different from those obtained from
the other. Thus the tracing of the respiration of a
person in hypnotic catalepsy showed smoothly-
rounded curves, while the tambour on the limb gave
an absolutely straight line; on the other hand, the
respiratory tracing from a man who imitated the
attitude showed sudden dives and jerks, becoming
sharper and sharper as moments passed, and the
tracing from the extended limb, at first fairly
straight, showed muscular tremors increasing in vio-
lence as the strain was prolonged. By these rigid
tests was fraud excluded, and the certainty of the
abnormal state established.

There are many ways in which the subject can be
thrown into the magnetic trance, such as holding the
hands and gazing fixedly into the eyes, making
downward passes over the face and trunk, placing
the thumb on the forehead while the fingers rest
lightly on the crown of the head etc. At the Salpêtrière, the operators, dealing with hysterical pa-

tients, have generally thrown the subject into the
rigid cataleptic state first, by a sudden noise, as a
blow and a gong, the flash of the electric light, or
other sudden sense-stimulus; a slower way is a continued slight stimulus, as looking upwards at a dark
or bright object—as in Braid's experiments.   The
subject may be made to pass from this cataleptic into
the lethargic state by further stimulus, and from this
into the "hypnotic," or lucid somnambulic, by light
friction of the scalp. The true hypnotic lethargy is
distinguished from catalepsy once more by respiratory tracings, those obtained from a subject passing
from lethargy into catalepsy showing the change in
the most unmistakable way, while a further check
has been secured by making tracings of the circu-
latory changes (by the use of the plethysmograph
and air-sphymograph), which are as marked as
those of the respiration.*

II.—The Facts.

As long ago as 1636 Daniel Schwenter hypnotised
a cock by tying its legs together, and placing its
beak at the end of a chalk line drawn along the
ground, an experiment still frequently repeated with
success; the tying of the legs is quite unnecessary
as the animal remains motionless if the beak be held

* See on these .tracings Binet and Féré's before-quoted work, pp.
120-134, where a number of these tracings are given; and, for greater
detail, P. Richer's "Etudes," pp. 337-355 and pp. 757-768.

on the line for a few minutes. Experiments on animals are satisfactory in so far as the possibility of fraud is here excluded, but of course only physical phenomena can be obtained from them. One word of warning is advisable, however to any who embark on this line of investigation, especially if they practise on the domestic cat or any of the canine race. There is a moment, just before success, when the animal is roused to rage—probably by terror—and will spring at the operator. Any start or blenching then means failure, and an ugly bite or scratch may be the result.

The facts of Animal Magnetism, for purposes of study, may be conveniently classed under three heads: 1. Its use as a therapeutic agent. 2. The exhaltation under it of the physical senses and mental capacities. 3. The control of the subject by the operator.

(1) *Its use as a therapeutic agent.*—The cures worked by Greatrakes, Mesmer, Du Potet, and other mesmerisers have already been alluded to, and during the present century a vast number of cures have been affected. Dr. Haddock records a case of blindness cured by him. A little girl of seven began to exhibit symptoms of cerebral affection, with partial paralysis, and eventually became totally blind; the child was brought to him, and by him submitted to a clairvoyante, who attributed the blindness to

the state of the roots of the optic nerve and the dis-
ordered condition of the nervous system. The child
was mesmerised every day, and at the end of three
weeks began to perceive light, improving gradually
until she was able to read large print.   This occurred at the close of the summer of 1849, and at
the end of 1850 the child had regained her sight,
but was somewhat short-sighted.* A famous case is
that of Harriet Martineau, who has left a record of
her own experience; she describes herself as reduced
to the last state of weakness, "a life passed between
my bed and the sofa."   All that medical skill could
do was done, and she was continually dependent on
opiates. She then put herself under mesmeric treatment, and "at the end of four months I was, as far
as my own feelings could be any warrant, quite
well." She describes her steady convalescence, "im-
proved composure of nerve and spirits," and the
help she found mesmerism to be in breaking off the
use of opiates.† Dr. Inglis, of Halifax, cured a girl,
eleven years old, of epileptic fits, by daily inducing
mesmeric sleep,‡ a form of sleep that is accompanied
with marked recuperation of the bodily energies.
Perhaps the most remarkable use of magnetism, under this head, is its employment as an anæsthetic.
One of the most famous operations performed on a

* Somnolism and Psychism," pp. 159, 160.
† Quoted in Newnham's "Human Magnetism," pp. 421-427.
‡ Ibid, pp. 139, 140.

mesmerised patient is the removal of the breast of an elderly French lady, Madame Plantin, for cancer, in 1829. Madame Plantin's physician, Dr. Chapelain, was in the habit of mesmerising her, and he found that she would placidly discuss the advisability of the proposed amputation when she was in the mesmeric trance, but shrank from it, when awake, with "the most intense anguish and apprehension." M. Jules Cloquet, an eminent surgeon of Paris, was chosen as operator, and found his patient in the mesmeric trance on his arrival. "She spoke calmly of the intended operation; removed her own dress to expose her bosom to the surgeon's knife; and during the operation, which lasted about a quarter of an hour, she conversed freely with the surgeon, and the physician, who was seated by her, supporting the arm of the diseased side, without exhibiting the slightest pain or consciousness of what was going on." She was kept under mesmerism for two days, and the wound began to heal in a healthy manner; but the patient died fourteen days later from another disease.* In 1851 Broca and Follin mesmerised a woman to make an incision in an abscess, and Guêrineau, of Poitiers, amputated the thigh of a hypnotised patient.† It is obvious that this use of hypnotism might prove most serviceable in cases in

* "Somnolism and Hypnotism," pp. 45, 46.
† "Animal Magnetism," by Binet and Féré, p. 77.

which chloroform cannot be employed without danger to life.

Carl Hansen has used mesmerism for the cure of nervous diseases of all sorts, for destroying by suggestion rooted ideas amounting to mania, for calming the insane in fits of fury, etc., etc. In India, where climatic influences are most favourable to the production of mesmeric phenomena, and among the sensitive Hindus, Colonel Olcott has cured diseases literally by the hundred, paralysis, blindness, deafness, dumbness, rheumatism, and so on. The use of clairvoyance in the diagnosis and cure of disease will be mentioned further on.

2) *The exaltation of the physical senses and mental capacities.*—This class of cases is full of instruction for the psychologist, for here, if anywhere, he can study mental phenomena apart from normal conditions, though if he insists on invariably connecting states of consciousness with cell-vibrations, he will find himself in parlous difficulties.

The quickening of the senses and of the mental capacities belongs to the lucid somnambulic condition, not to that of lethargy. Binet and Féré say:

The state of the senses in hypnotic subjects ranges from anæsthesia to hyperæsthesia. During lethargy all the senses are suspended, with the occasional exception of the sense of hearing, which is sometimes retained, as it is in natural sleep. During catalepsy, the special senses are partially awake; the muscular sense, in particular, retains all its activity. Finally, in somnambulism the senses are not merely awake, but quickened to an extraordinary degree. Subjects feel the cold produced by breathing from the mouth at a distance of several yards (Braid). Weber's compasses, applied to the skin, produce a two-fold sensation, with a deviation of 3°, in regions where, during the waking state, it should be necessary to give the instrument a deviation of 18° (Berger). The activity of the sense of sight is sometimes so great that the range of sight may be doubled, as well as the sharpness of vision. The sense of smell may be developed so that the subject is able to discover by its aid the fragments of a visiting card which had been given to him to smell before it was torn up (Taguet). The hearing is so acute that a conversation carried on on the floor below may be overheard.*

Many of the extraordinary phenomena of clairvoyance appear to be directly related to this abnormal sensibility, the bounds of time and space being ultimately completely cast aside. A girl of seventeen, named Jane Rider, was very carefully observed by her medical attendant, Dr. Belden; he found—amid many other curious facts—that she could read and write with two wads of cotton-wool over her eyes, coming down to the middle of the cheek, in close contact with the nose, and closely bound with a large black handkerchief; thus blinded, she on one occasion wrote the words *Stiff Billy*, and then correctly dotted the *i* in each word, wrote *Springfield* under them, leaving out the *l*, and went back and put the missing letter in the right place.† Schelling, the German philosopher, relates a case he observed,

* "Animal Magnetism," pp. 134, 135.
† "Isis Revelata," vol. i., P. 377.

in which a clairvoyante began to cry, and said that the death of a member of the family had taken place at a distance of 150 leagues. She added that the letter announcing the death was on its way. On awaking, she remembered nothing and was quite bright and cheerful, but when again hypnotised she again wept over the death. A week later, Schelling found her crying, with a letter beside her on the table announcing the death, and on asking whether she had previously heard of his illness, she answered that she had heard no such news of him, and that the intelligence was quite unexpected.* Similar stories, vouched by names of the highest character, may be found by the dozen in books dealing with these phenomena, so there is nothing unjustifiable in the statement of Schopenhauer: "Who at this day doubts the facts of animal magnetism and its clairvoyance, is not to be called sceptical, but ignorant."†

A use of clairvoyance that has been too much neglected is its employment for the diagnosis of obscure forms of disease. The Madame Plantin alluded to above had a daughter, Madame Lagandré, who was a clairvoyante, and who visited her mother shortly before her death; she described the state of the right lung and heart, the stomach and liver, describing the right lung as being shrivelled up, compressed, and no longer breathing, and saying

* Ibid, vol. i., pp. 89, 92.   † "Versuch über Geistersehen."

that there was water in the cavity of the heart. A post-mortem examination was conducted on Madame Plantin's body in the presence of Dr. Drousart, M. Moreau—secretary to the surgical section of the Royal Academy of Medicine, Paris—and Dr. Chapelain, by MM. Cloquet and Pailloux. The state of the organs was found to exactly bear out the somnambule's description.* Dr. Haddock's somnambule, Emma, constantly diagnosed diseases for him, and indicated appropriate remedies, which were applied with great success.† Here, again, a mass of evidence is available for all who desire to further study the subject. Dr. Sprengel, Dr. Brandis, Dr. Georget, and other physicians equally eminent, have advocated the employment of somnambulists for the diagnosis of disease.

Passing from the senses to the more intellectual faculties we find that the memory becomes, to an extraordinary degree, retentive under hypnotism: a poem was read over to a hypnotised subject and she was awakened; she could not remember it, but on being again hypnotised she repeated it correctly. At the Salpêtrière a hypnotised subject gave the *menu* of dinners she had eaten a week previously. A hypnotised girl, in Charcot's room, was asked the

---

* See "Isis Revelata," vol. ., pp. 87-89; and "The Philosophy of Mysticism," Du Prel, vol. i., pii 236. A full account is given by Dr. Haddock, in "Somnolism and Psychism," pp. 54-56.

† "Somnolism and Psychism," chap. 7.

name of a man who entered the room, and at once answered, "M. Parrot." She was awakened and again questioned, but said she did not know him; at last, after looking at him for a long time, she said that she thought he was a physician at the *Enfantes assistés* (as was the fact). It appeared that she had been at the Refuge when she was two years old, but had naturally forgotten the physician: hypnotised, her memory promptly recalled even his name.* Similarly, the general mental capacity is quickened. The girl before mentioned, Jane Rider, blindfolded carefully, was asked to learn backgammon; she consented, knowing nothing of the game, learned it rapidly, and won the sixth game from an experienced player; awakened, she was asked to play, but said she had never seen the game, and she could not even set the men.† Dr. Abercrombie gives a long account of a girl, whom he describes as "when awake, a dull, awkward girl, very slow in receiving any kind of instruction, though much care was bestowed upon her"; but, when in the somnambulic condition, "she often descanted with the utmost fluency and correctness on a variety of topics, both political and religious, the news of the day, the historical parts of Scripture, public characters, and particularly the characters of members of the family

* Binet and Féré, pp. 136, 137.
† "Isis Revelata," vol. i., pp. 381, 382.

and their visitors. In these discussions she showed the most wonderful discrimination, often combined with sarcasm, and astonishing powers of mimicry. Her language through the whole was fluent and correct, and her illustrations often forcible and even eloquent. She was fond of illustrating her subjects by what she called a fable, and in these her imagery was both appropriate and elegant.''*

Such facts as these, which might be multiplied a hundredfold, should surely give pause to the Materialist, who will have thought to be nothing more than the result of the vibration of brain-cells; and if it be objected that, numerous as they are, these cases are yet exceptional and abnormal, we may fitly reply with Herschell: ''The perfect observer will have his eyes, as it were opened that they may be struck at once with any occurrence which, according to received theories, ought not to happen, for these are the facts which serve as clues to new discoveries.''†

(3) *The control of the subject by the operator.*— Here we come to the very heart of our question: to the most marvellous facts, the most serious dangers, and the phenomena most luminous for psychological discovery. This control of the hypnotised person by the hypnotiser is absolute, complete; as Dr. Richer

* "On the Intellectual Powers," pp. 296 *et seq.* Quoted in "Isis Revelata."

† "Preliminary Discourse on the Study of Natural Philosophy," sec. 127.

says, "The somnambulist . . . is no longer a simple machine. He is the slave of the will of another, the veritable *subject* of the operator. His automatism consists in servitude and obedience."[*]

Take first the senses. These can be so deceived as to sensate when there is no object of sensation, to remain passive when stimuli are applied. The patient is plunged in the hypnotic trance; he is told that he will see or not see, feel or not feel, a certain thing; he is then awakened, but the "suggestion" continues to dominate his intelligence, and, apparently acting freely, he blindly obeys. A hypnotised patient was told that a bird was on her knee, and on awaking she stroked and caressed it;[†] another was told that he had a lamp-shade placed between his hands, and on awaking he pressed his hands against the imaginary object and could not bring them together;[‡] a card was placed on a sheet of white paper, and an imaginary line drawn round the card on the paper with a blunt pointer, the pointer not quite touching the paper; when the subject awoke, the blank paper was given to her, and she saw the rectangle which had *not* been traced on it, and, on request, she folded the paper along the lines she saw, folding it to the exact size of the card.[§]

---

* "Etudes Cliniques, " p. 789.
† Ibid, p. 645.
‡ Binet and Féré, p. 213.
§ "Etudes Cliniques," p. 723.

The reality of the hallucination is strikingly shown by an experiment in which the subject was told that there was a portrait on a piece of blank cardboard; when she awoke she saw the portrait, when the cardboard was turned round the portrait was reversed, and when the other side of the cardboard was shown nothing was seen, although these changes of position were made out of sight of the patient.* Even more strange is it that such an imaginary portrait is seen magnified or diminished if looked at by the subject through an opera-glass. A patient was told that Dr. Charcot was present when he was absent, and on awaking she addressed him; while another, told that she could not see Dr. F., was unable to see him though in the room; she was given permission to leave the room, and Dr. F. placed himself in front of the door; she came in contact with him without seeing him, and after making a second attempt to reach the door became alarmed at a resistance in the air she could not understand, and refused to make any further effort; a hat placed on his head was seen by her as suspended in the air, and a cloak he put on moved about "like a hollow puppet."† I have myself been rendered invisible in this way, with the quaintest of results.

Another class of experiments is the formation of hallucinatory complex visions. A patient was told

* Binet and Féré, p. 224.
† Ibid, pp. 306-308.

that Paradise was before her, and she described the Virgin Mary, the saints and angels, it being noticed that the details of the vision in such cases varied with the belief and fancy of the subject.* Another was made to see the devil; "she drew herself up, anger in her face, in a superb pose of wrath and defiance. At the end of a few moments she uttered a piercing cry, and fled to the other end of the room."† Another, described as a "very respectable woman, the mother of a family and very pious," was made to assume in turns the characters of a peasant, an actress—a very free-spoken one—a general, and a priest. We have here the explanation of many of the visions of nuns and others in a highly excited nervous condition; the upward-turned and fixed gaze is the very one used by Braid for self-hypnotisation, and the dominant idea would take the place of the suggestion.

Absolute physical lesion can be caused by suggestion. Charcot and his assistants have produced the physical effects of a burn by suggesting to a hypnotised patient that she has burned herself; a doctor traced some words with a blunt probe on the arm of a hypnotised subject, and told him that at four o'clock blood would come out on the lines traced; at the time named the words appeared in red, with

* "Etudes Clinques," pp. 669 and 790.
† Ibid, p. 699, *note*.

minute spots of blood. Surely we have here the explanation of the appearance of the "sacred stigmata" on ecstatic men and women meditating long on the passion of Christ.

Just as the body can be affected and the senses deceived, so can the inner sanctuary of the mind be invaded, and the will of the operator take the place of the paralysed volition of the subject. Then comes the possibility of suggesting action, action that may be either criminal or salutary. At the Salpêtrière and elsewhere suggestion of crime has been made and carried out after the subject has awaked; thus, told to poison one of the doctors with a glass containing water, the subject, after awaking, took the glass to him and offered him the water, with the remark that it was a hot day. Others have been made to stab one of the doctors present, to steal, etc.* Considerable cunning is evinced in the way in which the suggestion is carried out, so that the person under control becomes a criminal of an especially dangerous type; the more so that the hypnotiser can at will destroy all memory alike of the suggestion and of the act. So serious to society has this new peril been considered, that both in Russia and in Germany a law has been passed forbidding the practice of hypnotism by any but duly

* Binet and Féré, pp. 286-291.

authorised persons—a law which it is absolutely impossible to enforce.

On the other hand, suggestion may be used for the most beneficial purposes. At Nancy, Dr. Liébault and his colleagues have used it to promote moral action and to check criminal propensities; and, lately, the Rev. Mr. Tooth, of Croydon, has cured by suggestion confirmed dipsomaniacs. He suggests to them, while in the hypnotic trance, that drink is unpleasant to them, that it is nauseous and will make them sick; and in the waking state it has this effect upon them, so that they shrink from it with loathing. Truly there is here a mighty power for weal or woe, according as it is used by pure or corrupt hands.

III.—THE EXPLANATION.

To the great majority of people the above facts are inexplicable, and it is noteworthy that the French experimenters offer no explanation of the facts they record. The explanation which I suggest, as a Theosophist, will be only a possible hypothesis for most of my readers, and will be promptly rejected by such of these as are Materialists.

We must now distinguish between Magnetism and Hypnotism, which, though closely allied by the phenomena they produce, are yet distinct in the agency employed. Animal Magnetism is, in its nature, nearly related to Mineral Magnetism, and is visible to the sensitive as light, as is the latter. Baron Reichenbach's famous researches proved that persons in a hyperæsthetic state could, when placed in a perfectly dark room, see a magnet by the luminosity surrounding it, a luminosity specially marked at the poles.* He found also that a similar luminosity is visible from the human hands, "brushes" being perceptible coming from the points of the fingers. This observation has been frequently repeated with clairvoyants, and the name of odyle, or odic force, has been given to this human magnetism. The reality of this current from the body was curiously shown by the behaviour of a cat with Emma, Dr. Haddock's sensitive; the cat jumped on Emma's lap when she had been mesmerised, and she began to stroke its head with her right hand. "The cat instantly began to evince signs of fear or pain, and to cry in a peculiar half-piteous, half-savage tone." The experiment was repeated with other cats and kittens, but some difficulty was experienced, "as the animals always became savage, and endeavoured to bite." When Emma was "away," *i.e.,* in the lucid somnambulic state, the left hand similarly affected the cat, showing that the currents in the body were reversed.†

* "Physico-Physiological Researches in the Dynamics of Magnetism, etc., in their Relation to Vital Force." Translated from the German by John Ashburner, M.D. Ed. 1853.
† "Somnolism and Psychism," pp. 109-111.

No sign of any such current, or the physical action of one human organism on another, has been observed in connection with hypnotism; a certain stimulus applied to the nerves seems to set up a bodily condition which is peculiarly sensitive to either internal or external stimuli; in the latter case the will of the operator comes in as the active agent.

There is little doubt that the ganglionic, or sympathetic, nervous system plays a great part in somnambulic phenomena, appearing indeed to act as the brain of the Sleep-Consciousness. In an account given in the *Lancet** of an tIalian woman who suffered from catalepsy, it is stated that the patient heard nothing by the ear, but "the lowest whisper, directed on the hollow of the hand, or sole of the foot, on the pit of the stomach, or along the traject of the sympathetic nerve," was perfectly heard. Mr. Colquhoun remarks "in many cases of catalepsy and somnambulism the usual organs of the senses have been found to be entirely dormant, and the seat of general sensibility transferred from the brain to the region of this ganglion, or *cerebrum abdominale*."† Du Prel remarks:

Now, as waking consciousness proceeds parallel with corresponding changes of the senses of the brain, so the transcendental psychological functions seem to be parallel with corresponding changes in the ganglionic system, whose central seat,

* Vol. xxiii., pp. 663 *et seq.*
† "Isis Revelata," vol. ii., p. 153.

the solar plexus, was already called by the ancients the seat of the belly. With a somnambule of the physician Petitin, the pit of the stomach protruded like a ball. Bertrand's somnambule said, pointing to her stomach, she had something there which spoke, and of which she could enquire. . . . A somnambule with Werner more particularly described the dualism of brain and solar plexus, as it reveals itself on the transition of somnamublism. Before her senses were suppressed, but while she was already gravitating towards somnambulism, she said: "Where am I? I am not at home in the head. There is a strange struggle between the pit of the stomach and the head; both would prevail, both see and feel. That cannot be; it is a tearing asunder. It is as if I must send down the head into the stomach if I would see anything. The pit of the stomach pains me if I think above; and yet down there it is not clear enough. I must wonder, and that with the head, over the new disposition of the stomach." *

It is held by many, and I think rightly, that the cerebrum is one pole of the human magnet, and the plexus solaris the other, although Reichenbach— from insufficient data, as it seems to me—contended that this axis is only secondary, and that the primary axis is transverse.

If we now examine the human consciousness, we shall find it broadly divided into two, the Sleeping and the Waking; all mesmeric, clairvoyant, hypnotic phenomena belong to the former, and the more complete the quiescence imposed on the bodily functions, the more vivid and intense are the activities of the "Sleep-Consciousness." One other point of grave significance should be noted: the hypnotised person

* "Philosophy of Mysticism," vol. i., pp. 170, 171.

on awaking knows nothing, save rarely, of what happened in the hypnotic trance; but "when he is
asleep his memory embraces all the facts of his
sleep, of his waking state, and of previous hypnotic
sleeps."* This Sleep-Consciousness, as seen at work
in the somnambulic state, has a memory to which
the waking memory is forgetfulness, can see in defiance of space and material obstruction, is keenly intellectual where the waking brain is dull, is to the
Waking-Consciousness as a giant beside a dwarf.
What is it, this luminous Eidolon which shines out
the more brightly as the bodily frame is unconscious?
I answer: it is the Inner Self, the true individuality,
the higher Ego, which dwells in the body as the
flame in the lamp, sending into the outer world such
shafts of its radiance as can pierce its covering.

This Consciousness of man is able to impress his
physical brain and so become the Waking-Consciousness, just so far as physical conditions admit; what
the Germans call the psycho-physical threshold divides, as it were, this Consciousness into two, not
really dividing the Consciousness, but dividing off
the amount it can impress on the physical organism
from that which the physical organism is incapable
of receiving. Of all that is below this threshold,
the physical organism remains unconscious. The
contents of the Waking-Consciousness are, then, only

* Binet and Féré, p. 135.

part of the contents of the Total Consciousness, and, indeed, a comparatively small part thereof. Now this threshold is variable, and varies with the physical condition; and the more sensitive the nervous system, the more outward stimuli are removed or the senses dulled to their reception, the more does this threshold sink, unveiling the contents of the Total, the Real Consciousness. So far as the second class of phenomena is concerned, the exaltation of the senses and of the mental capacities, this hypothesis, worked out, will be found to be thoroughly explanatory. Once realise that the physical organs of sense are, as has been well said, barriers between the inner senses, the perceptive faculties of the Inner Self, and the objective world, that they are *organs*, not faculties, and it will be seen how their paralysis may make way for the inner senses to function.

The third class of phenomena, the control of the individual by the operator, turns once more, as to the hallucinations, on this movability of the threshold of sensation. Let us conceive of existence as one vast line, which has spirit or force for one end and grossest matter for the other end, all phenomena, "material" and "immaterial," ranging between these, not differing in essence, but in degree of condensation—so that condensed force would present itself as matter, rarefied matter as force. Let

us consider, next, that the universe, to us, exists as
conceived, our conception depending on the impression made by it on us through our senses. It will
at once be seen that a thing will present itself to
us as matter or as force according as it can or cannot affect our senses; that which affects the senses
directly will be recognised as matter, that which is
only apprehended by the mind through its effects
will be recognised as force. Whether the mental
presentment of a thing is material or immaterial will
depend, then, on our sensibility and not on the thing
itself, and the variation of our threshold of sensibility will transfer a thing from the matter-world
to the force-world, and *vice versa.** Thus to our
normal senses the attraction between the magnet
and all iron within the magnetic field is invisible,
and we speak of the force of attraction: to the sensitive or the somnambulist this force is visible as light.
The senses condition the nature of the perception.
Then, to abnormally sharpened senses, a thought may
become a material object, force-vibrations becoming
visible, *i.e.,* appearing as matter. But if this be so,
the "hallucination" of the somnambulist, who sees
a bird or a lamp-shade at the suggestion of the hypnotiser, results from her threshold of sensibility being so shifted that the normally immaterial thought
becomes to her material.

* See the admirable argument on this subject in Du Prel's "Philosophy of Mysticism," vol. ii., pp. 130-135.

This hypothesis does not explain the paralysis of vision as to objects, or parts of objects, which is one of the most startling of hypnotic phenomena. For elucidation of this I am somewhat at a loss. Patanjali speaks of the possibility of disconnecting "that property of Satwa which exhibits itself as luminousness" from the organ of sight of the spectator;* and the ancient Hindus held that there was this connection, so to speak, between the seer and the object seen. That an object *can* be made to disappear, I know, having seen it done and having been made myself to disappear; for the explanation, I am still groping.

The control of acts is easier to understand, for here one can see that the Ego of the hypnotised person may, as it were, be thrust aside and the Ego of the hypnotiser take its place, using the brain and the limbs of the subject as its tool. Be this as it may, the recognition of this true Ego, this Inner Self, acting in and through the body, but its master, not its product, offers, at least, a hopeful path to the solution of the abstruse problems that face us. That psychology should become in the West, as in the East, an experimental science, must be the wish of every patient searcher after Truth.

* Yoga Aphorisms." Ed. 1889, p. 31.

Memory

Reprinted from "Lucifer," November, 1889.

Memory is but a function of the mind, and the answer given to the question, "What is Memory?" must turn on the answer given to the larger question, "What is Mind?" "Is there a Self or Ego, of which the mind, as we know it, is a part; or is mind only the outcome of matter in motion, so that the Self has no real existence? Is mind anything more than an everchanging succession of perceptions and congeries of perceptions, and these the outcome of nervous activity responding to stimuli peripheral and central? Or is it a definite mode of being, with perceptions *et hoc genus omne* as material on which it works; with the faculties whereby it perceives, reproduces, recollects, conceives; but no more as a whole to be identified with its functional activities than the body as a whole consists of eating, breathing or digesting?"

The famous argument of Hume, in the fifth and sixth sections of *A Treatise on Human Nature*, Part

IV., will be familiar to the student: but I may here recall the results of his introspection:

For my part, when I enter most intimately into what I call myself, I always stumble on some particular perception or other, of heat or cold, light or shade, pain or pleasure. I never can catch *myself* at any time without a perception. When my perceptions are removed for any time, as by sound sleep, so long am I insensible of *myself*, and may truly be said not to exist. And were all my perceptions removed by death, and I could neither think nor feel, nor see, nor love, nor hate, after the dissolution of my body, I should be entirely annihilated, nor can I conceive what is further necessary to make me a perfect non-entity. If anyone, upon superior and unprejudiced reflection, thinks he has a different notion of *himself*, I must confess I can reason no longer with him. All I can allow him is, that he may be in the right as well as I, and that we are essentially different in this particular. He may, perhaps, perceive something simple and continued which he calls *himself;* though I am certain there is no such principle in me. I may venture to affirm of the rest of mankind, that they are nothing but a bundle or collection of different perceptions, which succeed each other with inconceivable rapidity, and are in a perpetual flux and movement.

Hume consequently denies the existence of the Self, and explains that the feeling of personal identity arises from the relations between the objects perceived.

But in reading the whole argument it is impossible to remain unconscious of the self-contradictory nature of the expressions used. "When *I* enter . . . *I* always stumble upon some perception." What is the "*I*" that stumbles on a perception, and is able to observe and to recognise it? Is it itself a perception? If so, of what? And can one perception in a "bundle" perceive other perceptions in the same bundle, and separating itself from its peers scrutinise the remainder and recognise them as a bundle? The argument implies something that observes the perceptions and that assigns to each its rightful name and place. Despite himself Hume cannot escape from the consciousness that he is other than his perceptions, and this universal result of introspection, the consciousness of the "I," betrays itself in the very argument aimed at its annihilation. The mind is no more identifiable with its organs than is the brain with the body of which it is a part. It depends on them for its living, and its functioning, but IT IS NOT THEY.

Consider an ordinary perception, say the perception of a chair. Can that perception cognise another, or be anything more than the perception of a chair? If the mind be only a bundle of perceptions, of what nature is the perception that can cognise all the rest? can set itself apart from and above all the rest, and say, "You are a perception of cold, and you of heat, and you of pain, and you of pleasure?" This perception of perceptions is not very different from the Self that is denied. It is the Perceiver, not a perception.

Let anyone experiment on himself; let him shut

himself up alone, free from all interruption from without; let him patiently and steadily investigate his mental processes; he will find that the shifting contents of his consciousness are not *he;* that he is other than the feelings, the perceptions, the conceptions that pass before him; that they are his, not he, and that he can drive them away, can empty his mind of all save Self-consciousness, can, in the words of Patanjali, become a "spectator without a spectacle."

It may be urged that introspection often yields fallacious results, and that self-observation is the most difficult of all tasks. Granted. So may our senses mislead us, but they are the only guides to the objective world that we possess. Our recognition of their fallibility does not lead us to refuse to use them, but it makes us test their report to the best of our ability, and compare them with the common sense of our race. And so with the result of our inner senses, we test them, compare their reports with those of others; and I venture to say that the common sense (I use the words in the philosophical meaning, the *sensus communis*) of mankind reports the existence of the Self, the permanent Ego amid all the flux of percepts and concepts, and that its existence is as certain as any existence around us in the Object World.

But we shall judge erroneously of the Ego if we

only take into account the every-day mental processes, and limit its extent to the extent of the normal waking consciousness. And I know of no study that can throw more light on our true Self than the study of Memory, for its phenomena prove to us that Consciousness is something far wider than the consciousness of the moment, as Energy, in the physical world, is something more than the forces acting at any given instant of time. Analogy is often useful as throwing light into obscure places, and analogy may serve us here. Physicists speak of Energy as kinetic and potential, the active and the latent. So Consciousness may be active or latent, and the latter division is for each individual the greatèr of the twain. We "forget" as the phrase goes, more than we "remember"; but the "forgotten" has not really passed out of the Consciousness, though it has become latent, any more than force is absent from the avalanche hanging quiescent on the side of a mountain. The forgotten can be recalled to the active consciousness, and may revolutionise a life as the avalanche may be set free and expand its stored-up energy in laying desolate the valley homes. No force can be annihilated on the physical plane, and no experience destroyed on the mental. That which the normal waking consciousness retains depends on the Attention, but a name for a phase of Will. That which is best remembered is that which has struck us vividly, *i.e.*, that which has arrested and fixed our attention, or that which has been often repeated so that our attention has been frequently directed to it; in every case the Will lies at the root of the retention. Everything that once enters into Consciousness leaves thereon its trace; the mind is thereby modified, as Patanjali would phrase it. If this be so the traces should be recoverable, and on this we must challenge the phenomena of Memory.

Let us note, at the commencement, that Memory has two chief divisions—Reproduction and Recollection. Reproduction may occur without Recollection, and then no recognition will ensue. Memory reproduces the image of past perceptions; it will appear to consciousness as new, unless recollection accompanies the reproduction, and instances of this are on record.

"Maury relates that he once wrote an article on political economy for a periodical, but the sheets were mislaid and, therefore, not sent off. He had already forgotten everything that he had written when he was requested to send the promised article. On re-undertaking the work, he thought he had found a completely new point of view for the subject; but when, some months later, the missing sheets were found, it appeared, not only that there was nothing new in his second essay, but that he had re-

peated his first ideas in almost the same words."*
Leibnitz is quoted by Du Prel as giving an analagous
instance: "I believe that dreams often renew old
thoughts. When Julius Scaliger had celebrated in
verse all the famous men of Verona, there appeared
to him in dream one who gave the name of Brugnolus, a Bavarian by birth, who had settled at
Verona, complaining that he had been forgotten.
Julius Scaliger did not recollect to have heard him
spoken of, but upon this dream made elegiac verses
in his honour. Afterwards his son, Joseph Scaliger,
being upon a journey through Italy learned that
formerly there had been at Verona a celebrated
grammarian or critic of that name, who had con-
tributed to the restoration of learning in Italy."†
The explanation suggested by Leibnitz is that Scaliger had heard of Brugnolus, but had forgotten
him; in the dream reproduction took place but was
not accompanied by recollection, so that the name
and character appeared new to Scaliger, and he
failed to recognise the dream-presented image. It
is impossible to say how much of our dreams may
be of this character, and how often the absence of
recognition may bestow on them the appearance of
revelation. We find ourselves in some place that
we have dreamed of, and recognise as real our sur-

* Maury, "Le Somneil et les Réves," p. 440, quoted by Du Prel,
"Philosophy of Mysticism," English trans., vol. ii., p. 13.
  † Ibid., pp. 14, 15.

roundings. Searching our waking consciousness in vain for some record, we rashly conclude that the dream has depicted in some mysterious way an environment unknown to us; whereas it is far more probable that memory has reproduced in our sleeping consciousness the images of perceptions long since forgotten, and recollection failing, they pass before the mind as new.

To return to the statement that "everything that has once entered consciousness leaves thereon its trace." In the article on "Memory of the Dying," in *Lucifer,* Vol. V., some examples were given of the remarkable reproduction at the end of life of events and surroundings of childhood, and almost everyone must have come across instances of aged persons who recall with extreme vividness the trivial occurrences of their youth. Dr. Winslow* remarks on some instances in which, "in a very advanced life, the faculty of memory exhibits an extraordinary degree of elasticity and a surprising amount of vigour. . . . A charming illustration of this fact occurs in the life of Niebhur, the celebrated Danish traveller. When old, blind, and so infirm that he was able only to be carried from his bed to his chair, he used to describe to his friends the scenes which he had visited in his early days with wonderful minuteness and vivacity. When they expressed their

* "Diseases of the Brain and Mind," pp. 286, 287.

astonishment at the vividness of his memory, he explained 'that as he lay in bed, all visible objects shut out, the pictures of what he had seen in the East continually floated before his mind's eye, so that it was no wonder that he could speak of them as if he had seen them yesterday. With like vividness the deep intense sky of Asia, with its brilliant and twinkling hosts of stars, on which he had so often gazed by night, or its lofty vault of blue by day, was reflected in the hours of stillness and darkness on his inmost soul.' ''

Yet more remarkable as a proof that that which has passed out of ordinary consciousness is not destroyed, are the many cases on record describing the strange revival of memory, just ere consciousness becomes latent, which is one of the most marked phenomena of drowning. I select the following from Du Prel:*

At the approach of death, also, the extraordinary exaltation of memory, connected with a change in the measure of time, has been frequently observed. Fechner† relates the case of a lady who fell into the water and was nearly drowned. From the moment when all bodily movement ceased till she was drawn out of the water about two minutes elapsed, during which, according to her own account, she lived again through her whole past, the most insignificant details of it being represented in her imagination. Another instance of the same mental action in which the events of whole years were crowded

* Vol. I., pp. 92, 93.
† "Zentralblatt für Anthropologie und Naturwissenschaft," Jahrgang, 1863, 774.

together is described by Admiral Beaufort from his own experience. He had fallen into the water, and had lost his
(normal) consciousness. In this condition ''thought rose after
thought, with a rapidity of succession that is not only inde-
scribable, but probably inconceivable by anyone who has not
himself been in a similar situation.'' At first, the immediate
consequences of his death to his family were presented to him;
then, his regards turned to the past: he repeated his last cruise,
an earlier one in which he was shipwrecked, his schooldays, the
progress he then made, and the time he had wasted, even all
his small childish journeys and adventures. ''Thus travelling
backwards, every incident of my past life seemed to me to
glance across my recollection in retrograded succession, *not,
however, in mere outline,* as here stated, but the picture *filled
up* with every minute and collateral feature; in short, the
whole period of my existence seemed to be placed before me
in a kind of *panoramic review,* and every act of it seemed to be
accompanied by a consciousness of right and wrong, or by
some reflection on its cause or its consequences. Indeed, many
trifling events, which had long been forgotten, then crowded
into my imagination, and with the character of recent famili-
arity.''* In this case, also, but two minutes at the most had
passed before Beaufort was taken out of the water.

The approach of death, like extreme old age, will
sometimes revive in the memory the impressions of
childhood to the obliteration of more recent habits.
Dr. Winslow† quotes Dr. Rush as recording a statement of the Rev. Dr. Muhlenberg, of Lancaster,
U.S.A., who, ''alluding to the German emigrants
over whom he exercised pastoral care, observes, 'people generally pray shortly before death in their

* Haddock, "Somnolism and Psychism," p. 213.
† *Loc. cit.,* p. 320.

native language. This is a fact that I have found
true in innumerable cases among my German hearers,
although hardly one word of their native lanagage
was spoken by them in common life and when in
health.' ''

Passing attacks of disease will alter the contents
of memory in the most remarkable way, so that the
view seems well-nigh forced upon us that the consciousness retains *all* impressions, but that the
threshold below which all is latent, shifts, as it were,
up and down, now letting some images appear in the
active consciousness and now others. The following
three illustrative cases are from Dr. Winslow's
work.* ''Dr. Hutchinson refers to the case of a physician who had in early life renounced the principles
of the Roman Catholic Church. During an attack
of delirium which preceded his death he prayed only
in the forms of the Church of Rome, while all recollection of the prescribed formulæ of the Protestant
religion was effaced and obliterated from the mind
by the cerebral affection. A gentleman was thrown
from his horse while hunting. He was taken from
the field to a neighbouring cottage in a state of unconsciousness, and was subsequently removed to his
own residence. For the period of a week his life
was considered in imminent danger. When he was
sufficiently restored to enable him to articulate, he

* pp. 320, 321.

began to talk German, a language he had acquired in early life, but had not spoken for nearly twenty-five years. . . . A gentleman had a serious attack of illness. When restored, it was found that he had lost all recollection of recent circumstances, but had a lucid memory as to events that had occurred in *early life,* in fact, impressions that had long been forgotten were again revived. As this patient recovered his bodily health, a singular alteration was observed in the character of his memory. He again recollected *recent* ideas, but entirely forgot all the events of past years.''

Another class of proofs of the permanence of impressions of the consciousness may be drawn from the recorded cases of the exaltation of memory, which frequently accompanies disease and abnormal conditions of the nervous system. Du Prel has collected a large number of instances, from which I take the following:*

Coleridge mentions a maid-servant who, in the delirium of fever, recited long passages in Hebrew which she did not understand, and could not repeat when in health, but which formerly, when in the service of a priest, she had heard him deliver aloud. She also quoted passages from theological works, in Latin and Greek, which she only half understood, when the priest, as was his custom, read aloud his favourite authors when going to and from church.† A Rostock peasant, in a fever, suddenly recited the Greek words commencing the Gospel of S. John,

* *Loc. sit.,* vol. ii., pp. 19, 21, 28.
† Maudsley, "Physiology and Pathology of the Soul," p. 14.

which he had accidentally heard sixty years before; and Ben-
ecke mentions a peasant woman who, in a fever uttered Syriac,
Chaldean and Hebrew words which, when a girl, she had accidentally heard in the house of a scholar. . . .* A de-
ranged person, who was cured by Dr. Willis, said that in his
attacks his memory attained extraordinary power, so that
long passages from Latin authors occurred to him. . . .†
A girl of seven, employed as neatherd, occupied a room divided
only by a thin partition from that of a violin player, who often
gave himself up to his favourite pursuit during half the night.
Some months later, the girl got another place, in which she
had already been for two years, when frequently in the night
tones exactly like those of the violin were heard coming from
her room, but which were produced by the sleeping girl herself. This often went on for hours, sometimes with interrup-
tions, after which she would continue the song where she had
left off. With irregular intervals, this lasted for two years.
Then she also produced the tones of a piano which was played
in the family, and afterwards she began to speak, and held
forth with remarkable acuteness on political and religious subjects, often in a very accomplished and sarcastic way; she
also conjugated Latin, or spoke like a tutor to a pupil. In all
which cases this entirely ignorant girl merely reproduced what
had been said by members of the family or visitors.

I have quoted this last case in order to draw attention to the significant fact that sleep may cause
the shifting of the threshold, as well as sickness or
insanity.

Dr. Winslow‡ gives some cases of extraordinary
memory, characterising incipient brain-disease, and
he also records many curious instances of "double

* Radestock, "Schlaf und Traum," p. 136.
† Reil, "Raphsodien," p. 304.
‡ *Loc. cit.*, pp. 336-338.

consciousness,'' in which the patient practically lives a double life, remembering in each state only those incidents which occurred in it.* Here, again, we seem to be confronted with the shifting threshold as the only tenable hypothesis.

Persons under hypnotism frequently exhibit an extreme exaltation of memory, repeating long passages read to them but once, recalling with accuracy long past and trivial events, describing minutely the insignificant occurrences of many successive days. Many instances of this kind will be found by the student in Binet and Féré's *Animal Magnetism,* and in Dr. Richer's *Etudes sur la grande Hystérie.*

With this rough survey of the field of memory in our minds, we must seek for some hypothesis which will resume the facts, and which, tested by fresh experiments, will explain other memory-phenomena. I put Hume's hypothesis out of court, and proceed to consider the Materialistic and Theosophical Theories of memory, to answer the question whether memory is a function of matter in motion, or a faculty of the Self, the Ego, functioning *through* matter, but not resultant from it.

The Materialistic Theory of Memory. According to this theory memory, like all other mental functions, is the result of the vibrations of the brain nerve-cells, and may be expressed in terms of mat-

* pp. 332-336.

ter and motion. When a stimulus from the Object-World sets up a vibration in a sense-organ, that vibration is propagated as a wave from cell to cell of the nervous chain till it reaches its appropriate centre in the cerebrum. There arises the perception, the outcome of *mental* activity. This nervous action, once set up, tends to repeat itself more easily with each similar stimulus, the nervous energy following the path of least resistance, and each occurrence of the similar vibration making easier further repetition. Such a vibration having once been set up, it may recur in the absence of the external stimulus, and we have the idea in lieu of the sensation-perception. Whenever the nerve cells vibrate as they vibrated under the first stimulus, the idea recurs, and this recurrence is termed memory. Now, when the vibration is first set up it is at its strongest, and it is argued that this intensity of vibration lessens until it is not sufficient to affect the consciousness. Mr. James Ward writes:* "What now do we know of this central image in the intervals when it is not consciously presented? Manifestly our knowledge in this case can only be inferential at the best. But there are two facts, the importance of which Herbart was the first to see, from which we may learn something. I refer to what he calls the rising

* "Journal of Speculative Philosophy," vol. xvii., No. 2, quoted by Sully.

and falling of presentations. All presentations having more than a limited intensity rise gradually to a maximum and gradually decline; and when they have fallen below the threshold of consciousness altogether, the process seems to continue; for the longer the time that elapses before their "revival," the fainter they appear when revived, and the more slowly they rise. This evanescence is more rapid at first, becoming less as the intensity of the presentation diminishes. It is too much to say that this holds with mathematical accuracy, although Herbart has gone this length. Still, it is true enough to suggest the notion that an object, even when it is no longer able to influence attention, continues to be presented, though with ever less and less absolute intensity, till at length its intensity declines to an almost dead level just above zero." Put into the materialistic language this would be that the nervous elements vibrate at first strongly and continue to vibrate, with less and less vigour, until the vibration is insufficient to affect the consciousness, and the image sinks below the threshold. The vibrations go on, still diminishing, but *not* ceasing; if they cease the image is lost beyond revival; if they continue, however feebly, they may be reinforced and once more rise to an intensity which lifts them above the threshold of consciousness. Such reinforcement is due to association. As Sully puts it very clearly :*

In order to understand more precisely what is meant by the Law of Contiguous Association, we may let A and B stand for two impressions (percepts) occurring together, and *a* and *b* for the two representations answering to these. Then the Law asserts that when A (or *a*) recurs it will tend to excite or call up *b*; and similarly that the recurrence of B (or *b*) will tend to excite *a*. . . . . The physiological explanation of the association seems to be the fact that two nerve structures that have repeatedly acted together acquire a disposition to act in combination in the same way. This fact is explained by the hypothesis that such a conjoint action of two nerve centres somehow tends to fix the line of nervous excitation or nervous discharge when one centre is again stimulated in the direction of the other. In other words, paths of connection are formed between the two regions. But it may be doubted whether physiologists can as yet give a satisfactory account of the nervous concomitants of the associative process.

Lewes defines memory on the physiological side as "an organised tendency to react on lines previously traversed";† and Herbert Spencer relates each class of feelings to its own group of cells (vesicles) in the brain. He says:

If the association of each feeling with its general class answers to the localisation of the corresponding nervous action within the great nervous mass in which all feelings of that class arise, if the association of this feeling with its sub-class answers to the localisation of the nervous action within that part of this great nervous mass in which feelings of this sub-class arise, and so to the end with the smallest groups of feel-

* "Outlines of Psychology," pp. 236, 237.
† "The Physical Basis of Mind," p. 462.

ings and smallest clusters of nerve-vesicles; then, to what answers the association of each feeling with predecessors identical in kind? It answers to the re-excitation of the particular vesicle or vesicles which, when before excited, yielded the like feeling before experienced; the appropriate stimulus having set up in certain vesicles the molecular changes which they undergo when disturbed, there is aroused a feeling of the same quality with feelings previously aroused when such stimuli set up such changes in these vesicles. And the association of feeling with the preceeding like feelings corresponds to the physical re-excitation of the same structures.*

We are then to regard memory as the result of the re-excitation of visicles of the brain—the theory is clear and definite enough. Is it true?

The first difficulty that arises is the limited space available for the containment of these vesicles, and the consequent limitation of their number. It is true that their possible combinations may be practically infinite in number, but this does not help us; for they are to continually vibrate, however feebly, so long as an idea is capable of revival, and a vesicle vibrating simultaneously in some thousands of combinations would be in a parlous molecular condition. For all these combinations must exist simultaneously, and each must maintain its inter-related vibrations without cessation. Now, is this possible? It is true that from the vibrating strings of a piano you may get myriads of combinations of notes; but you cannot have all these combinations sounding

* "Principles of Psychology," vol. i., p. 258.

from the strings at the same time, some loud and some soft, some forcible and some feeble. By keeping the loud pedal down you may keep some combinations going for a short time, while you produce fresh vibrations; but what is the effect? A blurred confusion of sounds, causing an intolerable discord. If we are to explain memory under the laws of matter in motion, we must accept the consequences deducible from these laws, and these consequences are inconsistent with the facts of memory as we know them. Any attempt to represent clearly in consciousness the physical concomitants of memory as merely the outcome of vibrating nervous elements will prove to the student the impossibility of the hypothesis. The brain is a sufficiently wonderful mechanism as the organ of mind; as the creator of mind it is inconceivable.

Du Prel* helps us to realise the difficulties enveloping the Materialistic hypothesis. On this hypothesis "Memory would depend on material brain-traces, left behind by impressions; by the act of memory such traces are continually renewed, re-chiselled as it were, and so there arise well-worn tracks" [Herbert Spencer's "lines of least resistance"], "in which the coach of memory is conducted with especial facility." And he adds:

The deductions from this view had already been drawn by

* "Philosophy of Mysticism," vol. ii., pp. 108, 109.

the Materialists of the last century. Hook and others recognised that, since one-third of a second sufficed for the production of an impression, in 100 years a man must have collected in his brain 9,467,280,000 traces or copies of impressions, or, reduced by one-third for the period of sleep, 3,155,-
760,000; thus in fifty years, 1,577,880,000; further that, allow-
ing a weight of four pounds to the brain, and subtracting one
pound for the blood and vessels and another for the external
integument, a single grain of brain substance must contain
205,542 traces. . . . . Moreover, our intellectual life does not
consist in mere impressions; these form only the material of
our judgment. These brain-atoms do not help us to judgment,
notwithstanding their magical properties, so that we must suppose that whenever we form a sentence or a judgment the impressions are combined, like the letters in a compositor's box,
these atoms, however, being at the same time compositor and
box.

There is another result that would follow from
memory being only the outcome of vibrating cells,
and I may be permitted to quote it from my essay
on Hypnotism: ''Memory is the faculty which receives the impressions of our experiences and preserves them; many of these impressions fade away,
and we say we have forgotten. Yet it is clear that
these impressions may be revived. They are, therefore, not destroyed, but are so faint that they sink
below the threshold of consciousness, and so no
longer form part of its normal content. If thought
be but a 'mode of motion,' memory must be similarly regarded; but it is not possible to conceive that
each impression of our past life, recorded in consciousness, is still vibrating in the same group of

MEMORY249

cells, only so feebly that it does not rise over the threshold. For these same cells are continually being thrown into groupings for new vibrations, and these cannot all co-exist, and the fainter ones be each capable of receiving fresh impulse which may so intensify their motion as to raise them again into consciousness. Now if these vibrations=Memory, if we have only matter in motion, we know the laws of dynamics sufficiently well to say that if a body be set vibrating, and new forces be successively brought to act on it and set up new vibrations, there will not be in that body the co-existence of each separate set of vibrations successively impressed upon it, but it will vibrate in a way differing from each single set and compounded of all. So that memory as a mode of motion, would not give us the record of the past, but would present us with a new story, the resultant of all those past vibrations, and this would be ever changing, as new impressions, causing new vibrations, come in to modify the resultant of the whole.'' If the reader have in mind the phenomena of memory given in the earlier part of this essay; if he note that these seem to imply that we forget *nothing*, *i.e.*, that every vibration caused throughout the life persists; if, remembering this, he once more attempts to represent clearly in consciousness the brain-condition required by this theory, is it too much to say that he will be compelled to admit that it is inconceivable?

Nor can we forget that there is a certain race-memory, wrought into our physical organisms, which still further complicates the work to be accomplished by these over-burdened vesicles. This unconscious memory of the body, derived from physical inheritance, cannot be wholly thrown out of account when we deal with cell-vibrations.

The Theosophical Theory of Memory. Here I must guard myself. I cannot really put the Theosophical Theory, for I do not find it set out in any work that I have read. I can only suggest a theory, which seems to me, as a student of Theosophy, to be fairly deducible from the constitution of man as laid down in Theosophical treatises. We learn to distinguish between the true individuality, the Ego, and the temporary personality that clothes it. The Ego is the conscious, the thinking agent. It is the Ego of whom the mind forms part, one of whose functions is memory. Every event that occurs passes into the consciousness of the Ego and is there stored up; the Past is thus for it ever the present, since all is present in consciousness.* But how far the Ego can impress its knowledge on the brain of the physical organism with which it is connected,

---

* All is present in eternal ideation, or *Alaya* the universal soul and consciousness—we are taught; and the higher Ego (*Manas*) is the first-born of *Alaya* or Mahat, being called *Manasaputra*—"Son of Mind."

and thus cause this knowledge to enter the consciousness of the person concerned, must, in the
nature of the case, depend on the condition of the
organism at the moment, and the laws within which
it works . What we call the threshold of consciousness divides what is "remembered" from what is
"forgotten." All above the threshold is within the
personal consciousness, while all below this threshold is outside it. But this threshold belongs to the
personal consciousness, and—here is the significant
point—varies with the material conditions of the
moment. It is movable, not fixed, and the contents
of consciousness vary with the movement of the
threshold. Thus:

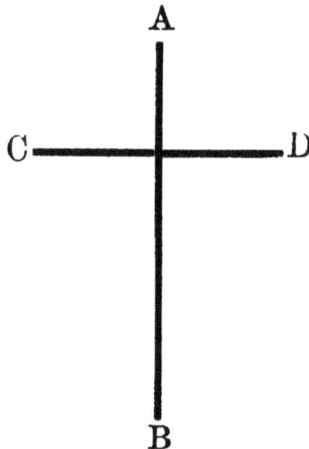

Let A B represent the consciousness of the Ego;
let C D represent the threshold of consciousness of
the person; of all above C D the person will be conscious, it will be impressed on the material brain;

of all below C D he will be unconscious. But if C D be movable upwards and downwards, the contents of his consciousness will vary with its movement, and he will remember or forget according as the idea is above or below this dividing line.*

Now, the condition of the organism is constantly varying; but there are two states of consciousness that occur in everyone and are clearly distinguishable—the waking consciousness and the dream consciousness. The contents of these differ to a remarkable extent, and they work under curiously different conditions. The waking consciousness works under conditions of time and space; the dream consciousness is free from them—it can live through years in a second of time, it can annihilate space in its movements. In the dream the place of the dreamer depends on his thought, he is where he thinks himself. Not only so, but the dream consciousness often retains events erased from the waking memory. Let the reader turn back to pp. 234, 235, and note the curious phenomena of reproduction without recollection in the dream state. It is an impossible theory that when the senses are closed to the Object-World, when the bodily functions have touched their lowest activity, then the Ego may be

* We have to exclude from this the impressions of a purely physical nature, such as enter in the category of *animal* perception and memory. Such impressions reach the Human Ego, and it cannot fail to note them; but they do not impress themselves indelibly on *its* consciousness, and can never, therefore, follow the Ego to Devachan.

able to impress on this negative organism far more of its own contents than it can impress upon it when in its more vigorous state? Does it not seem as though that which is below the threshold of the waking consciousness becomes that which is above the threshold of the dream consciousness, and as though the double life of waking and sleeping is but the activity of the one Ego working under the contrasted physical conditions?

If this be not so, we seem to be driven to the conception of a duality at the very centre of being; each man is not one, but twain, in the innermost recesses of consciousness.

On the other hand, the theory for which I contend leaves the individuality single, varying in its manifestations according to the physical conditions through which it works; and all the strange cases of double consciousness, which have so perplexed the physiologist and the psychologist, together with the phenomena of somnambulism, mesmerism, hypnotism, and similar conditions, fall into line as severally belonging to one of the two states of consciousness, the dream and the waking, the Ego working equally in either, but conditioned in turn by each.

"Ordinary sleep," as Du Prel says, "is a condition intermediate between waking and somnambulism, the latter being only its exaltation." In this connection these facts are to be noted: if we sleep lightly and dream, we remember our dreams; if we sleep more soundly, we sometimes remember the dream more vividly on waking, but in an hour or two we have completely forgotten it and cannot revive the memory try as we may; in deep sleep we dream, as has often been discovered by closely watching a person wrapped in profound slumber, but no trace remains on our waking memory. In somnambulism, which is closely allied to this deep sleep, no memory persists, as a rule, into the waking state. A person who is a somnambulist lives a double life: sleeping, he remembers his sleep experiences and sometimes his waking ones; waking, he remembers only his waking life. Occasionally, but only rarely, the golden bridge of memory spans the gulf between the waking and the somnambulic consciousness, dreams sometimes interposing as connecting link between the two. It must be remembered that a somnambulic, left to himself, will pass into ordinary sleep before awaking, and when this is the case dream may carry on memory of the somnambulic into the waking state.

Du Prel puts very clearly the existence of what he calls the "transcendental consciousness," which has much in common though it is not identical with, the Theosophical Ego.

There can be no right theory of remembering without the

right theory of forgetting.   The phenomenon of alternating consciousness shows this very clearly.   It is only when we know what has become of an impression when it is forgotten, that we can answer the question whence it comes to memory.   Now, what is the process of forgetting?   It is a disappearance from the normal sense-consciousness.   There can be no destruction of the impression, or its reproduction would be impossible.   Excluding the brain-trace theory, there must be a psychical organ, preserving *the faculty of reproduction*, even if the impression, as product of the *earlier* activity, should be destroyed. This organ, lying beyond the self-consciousness, belongs to the unconscious.   If, however, this organ had simply the latent faculty of reproduction, and did not rather draw into itself and preserve unchanged the impression as product, we should have again within this organ to distinguish between the conscious and the unconscious.   The hypothesis would thus explain nothing, the difficulty being merely pushed back and transposed. There is, therefore, no alternative but to say that this organ is not in itself at all unconscious, but only so from the standpoint of the sense-consciousness; that it is not merely a latent faculty of reproduction, but takes up into *its* consciousness the impression, as the latter disappears from the external consciousness.   By this admission of a transcendental consciousness. If a forgotten impression sank into a real unconscious, it would not be apparent how in memory this unconscious should suddenly become again conscious.   The forgotten, therefore, cannot cease to belong to a consciousness, and since forgetting is the disappearance from the sense-consciousness, we must admit the existence of a second.   And so, to say that an impression is forgotten is to say that it has passed over from the sense-consciousness to the transcendental.*

The answer to this that would leap to the lips of the Materialist is that the impression "goes" nowhither, any more than motion "goes" anywhere

* Vol. II., pp. 111-113.

when a wheel is stopped. But this obvious answer
leaves out important facts in the case. The motion
is changed into another form of physical energy, as
heat caused by the friction which stops it, and the
wheel cannot reproduce motion; the new impulse to
move must come from a living force without it.
Now the impression *is* revivable, without any external action, by Self-action, and the Materialist
theory of Memory implies its continual production
by ceaselessly vibrating vesicles, albeit the vibrations
be not vigorous enough to attract attention.

If we admit the existence of the Ego, personal
memory would be the power of the personal brain
to receive impressions from it; to respond, so to
speak, to the subtler vibrations of, perhaps, the
"thought-stuff" of which Clifford dreamed. Com-
paring the vibrations of our gross forms of matter
with the vibrations of the ether we can reason by
analogy to a form of matter as much subtler than
the ether as that is subtler than the nerve-matter of
our brain. There, indeed, may be the possibility of
vibrations such as are necessary to make our thought
process conceivable. At present, this can only be a
hypothesis to us, but it is a hypothesis which throws
light on this obscure subject, and may be provision-
ally accepted, until further researches prove or dis-
prove it.

Here will find their justification all attempts to

refine and increase the sensitiveness of the nerve matter of the brain, for increased delicacy will mean increased faculty of responding to the hyper-ethereal vibrations—that is, it will enable the Ego to impress on our personal consciousness more and more the contents of his own. By this theory we can understand the exalted mental faculties of the somnambulist, the tension of the nervous system rendering it more sensitive, *i.e.*, more responsive. By it also we can understand the danger of the ignorant striving after this abnormal condition, the nervous elements becoming exhausted by over-rapid discharge and excessive strain. ''Great wits to madness often are allied'' is only too true; the sensitiveness which is genius may easily pass into the hypersensitiveness that is insanity.

And so we reach the practical conclusion—to walk warily in these little-trodden realms, because there is danger; but to walk, for without the courage to face the darkness no light can come.

The Nature of Memory

Reprinted from "The Theosophical Review" for August and September, 1904.

The nature of memory is a problem which has been troubling theosophical students for many years, and perhaps I may only succeed in troubling them still further by offering a theory on the subject; on the other hand it is possible that I may succeed in helping them a little by the presentation of a view that is to myself helpful and clarifying.

What is memory? and how does it work? by what means do we recover the past, whether near or remote? For, after all, whether the past be near or remote, belonging to this or to any anterior life, the means which govern its recovery must be similar, and we require a theory which will include all cases of memory, and at the same time will enable us to understand each particular case.

The first step towards obtaining a definite and intelligible theory is a comprehension of our own composition, of the Self with its sheaths, and their interrelation. We must bear constantly in mind the facts that our consciousness is a unit, and that this unit of consciousness works through various sheaths, which impose upon it a false appearance of multiplicity. The innermost, or most tenuous, of the sheaths is inseparable from the unit of consciousness; in fact, it is this sheath which makes it a unit. This unit is the Monad, dwelling on the Anupâdaka plane; but for all practical purposes we may take it as the familiar Inner Man, the Tri-Atom, Atmâ-Buddhi-Manas, thought of as apart from the âtmic, buddhic and mânasic sheaths. This unit of consciousness manifests through, abides in, sheaths belonging to the five planes of its activity, and we call it the Self working in its sheaths.

We must think, then, of a conscious Self dwelling in vehicles that vibrate. The vibrations of these vehicles correspond, on the side of matter, with the changes in consciousness on the side of the Self. We cannot accurately speak of vibrations of consciousness, because vibrations can only belong to the material side of things, the form side, and only loosely can we speak of a vibrating consciousness. We have changes in consciousness corresponding with vibrations in sheaths.

The question of the vehicles, or bodies, in which consciousness, the Self, is working, is all-important as regards memory. The whole process of recovering more or less remote events is a question of picturing them in the sheath—of shaping part of the matter of the sheath into their likeness—in which

THE NATURE OF MEMORY

consciousness is working at the time. In the Self, as a fragment of the Universal Self—which for our purpose we can take to be the LOGOS, although in verity the LOGOS is but a portion of the Universal Self—is present everything; for in the Universal Self is present all which has taken place, is taking place, and will take place in the universe; all this, and an illimitable more is present in the Universal Consciousness. Let us think only of a universe and its LOGOS. We speak of Him as omnipresent and omniscient. Now, fundamentally, that omnipresence and omniscience are in the individualised Self, as being one with the LOGOS, but—we must put in here a but—with a difference; the difference consisting in this, that while in the separated Self as Self, apart from all vehicles, the omnipresence and omniscience reside by virtue of his unity with the One Self, the vehicles in which he dwells have not yet learned to vibrate in answer to his changes of consciousness, as he turns his attention to one or another part of his contents. Hence we say that all exists in him potentially, and not as in the LOGOS actually: all the changes which go on in the consciousness of the LOGOS are reproducible in this separated Self, which is an indivisible part of His life, but the vehicles are not yet ready as media of manifestation. Because of the separation of form, because of this closing in of the separate, or individualised,

Self, these possibilities which are within it as part of the Universal Self are latent, not manifest, are possibilities, not actualities. As in every atom which goes to the making up of a vehicle, there are illimitable possibilities of vibration, so in every separated Self there are illimitable possibilities of changes of consciousness.

We do not find in the atom, at the beginning of a solar system, an illimitable variety of vibrations; but we learn that it possesses a capacity to acquire an illimitable variety of vibrations; it acquires these in the course of its evolution, as it responds continually to vibrations playing upon its surface; at the end of a solar system, an immense number of the atoms in it have reached the stage of evolution in which they can vibrate in answer to any vibration touching them that arises within the system; then, for that system, these atoms are said to be perfected. The same thing is true for the separated, or individualised, Selves. All the changes taking place in the consciousness of the LOGOS which are represented in that universe, and take shape as forms in that universe, all these are also within the perfected consciousness in that universe, and any of these changes can be reproduced in any one of them. Here is memory: the re-appearance, the re-incarnation in matter, of anything that has been within that universe, and therefore ever *is*, in the consciousness of its LOGOS, and in the consciousness which are parts of His consciousness. Although we think of the Self as separate as regards all other Selves, we must ever remember it is inseparate as regards the ONE SELF, the LOGOS. His life is not shut out from any part of His universe, and in Him we live and move and have our being, open ever to Him, filled with His life.

As the Self puts on vehicle after vehicle of matter, its powers of gaining knowledge become, with each additional vehicle, more circumscribed but also more definite. Arrived on the physical plane, consciousness is narrowed down to the experiences which can be received through the physical body, and chiefly through those openings which we call the sense-organs; these are avenues through which knowledge can reach the imprisoned Self, though we often speak of them as shutting out knowledge when we think of the capacities of the subtler vehicles. The physical body renders perception definitive and clear much as a screen with a minute hole in it allows a picture of the outside world to appéar on a screen that would otherwise show a blank surface; rays of light are truly shut off from the screen, but by that very shutting off, those allowed to enter form a clearly defined picture.

Let us now see what happens as regards the physical vehicle in the reception of an impression and in the subsequent recall of that impression, *i.e.*, in the memory of it.

A vibration from outside strikes on an organ of sense, and is transmitted to the appropriate centre in the brain. A group of cells in the brain vibrates, and that vibration leaves the cells in a state somewhat different from the one in which they were previous to its reception. The trace of that response is a possibility for the group of cells; it has once vibrated in a particular way, and it retains for the rest of its existence as a group of cells the possibility of again vibrating in that same way without again receiving a stimulus from the outside world. Each repetition of an identical vibration strengthens this possibility, each leaving its own trace, but many such repetitions will be required to establish a self-initiated repetition; the cells come nearer to this possibility of a self-initiated vibration by each repetition compelled from outside. But this vibration has not stopped with the physical cells; it has been transmitted inwards to the corresponding cell, or group of cells, in the subtler vehicles, and has ultimately produced a change in consciousness. This change, in its turn, re-acts on the cells, and a repetition of the vibrations is initiated from within by the change in consciousness, and this repetition is a memory of the object which started the series of vibrations. The response of the cells to the vibration from outside, a response compelled by the laws of the physical universe, gives to the cells the power of responding to a similar impulse, though feebler, coming from within. A little power is exhausted in each moving of matter in a new vehicle, and hence a gradual diminution of the energy in the vibration. Less and less is exhausted as the cells repeat similar vibrations in response to new impacts from without, the cells answering more readily with each repetition.

Therein lies the value of the "without"; it wakes up in the matter, more easily than by any other way, the possibility of response, being more closely akin to the vehicles than the "within."

The change caused in consciousness, also, leaves the consciousness more ready to repeat that change than it was first to yield it, and each such change brings the consciousness nearer to the power to initiate a similar change. Looking back into the dawnings of consciousness, we see that the imprisoued Selves go through innumerable experiences before a Self-initiated change in consciousness occurs; but bearing this in mind, as a fact, we can leave these early stages, and study the workings of consciousness at a more advanced point. We must also remember that every impact, reaching the innermost sheath and giving rise to a change in con-

sciousness, is followed by a re-action, the change in
consciousness causing a new series of vibrations from
within outwards; there is the going inwards to the
Self, followed by the rippling outwards from the
Self, the first due to the object, and giving rise to
what we call a perception, and the second due to the
re-action of the Self, causing what we call a memory.

A number of sense-impressions, coming through
sight, hearing, touch, taste and smell, run up from
the physical vehicle through the astral to the mental.
There they are co-ordinated into a complex unity,
as a musical chord is composed of many notes. This
is the special work of the mental body: it receives
many streams and synthesizes them into one; it
builds many impressions into a perception, a thought,
a complex unity.

Let us try to catch this complex thing, after it
has gone inwards and has caused a change in consciousness, an idea; the change it has caused gives
rise to new vibrations in the vehicles, reproducing
those it had caused on its inward way, and in each
vehicle it reappears in a fainter form. It is not
strong, vigorous and vivid, as when its component
parts flashed from the physical to the astral, and
from the astral to the mental; it reappears in the
mental in a fainter form, the copy of that which the
mental sent inwards, but the vibrations feebler; as
the Self receives from it a re-action—for the im-

pact of a vibration on touching each vehicle *must* cause a re-action—that re-action is far feebler than the original action, and will therefore seem less "real" than that action; it makes a lesser change in consciousness, and that lessening represents inevitably a less "reality."

So long as the consciousness is too little responsive to be aware of any impacts that do not come through with the impulsive vigour of the physical, it is literally more in touch with the physical than with any other sheath, and there will be no memories of ideas, but only memories of perceptions, *i.e.*, of pictures of outside objects, caused by vibrations of the nervous matter of the brain, reproducing themselves in the related astral and mental matter. These are literally pictures in the mental matter, as are the pictures on the retina of the eye. And the consciousness perceives these pictures, "sees" them, as we may truly say, since the seeing of the eye is only a limited expression of its perceptive power. As the consciousness draws a little away from the physical, turning attention more to the modifications in its inner sheaths, it sees these pictures reproduced in the brain from the astral sheath by its own re-action passing outwards, and there is the memory of sensations. The picture arises in the brain by the re-action of the change in consciousness, and is recognised there. This recognition implies that the consciousness has withdrawn largely from the physical to the astral vehicle, and is working therein. The human consciousness is thus working at the present time, and is, therefore full of memories, these memories being reproductions in the physical brain of past pictures, caused by re-actions from consciousness. In a lowly evolved human type, these pictures are pictures of past events in which the physical body was concerned, memories of hunger and thirst and of their gratification, of sexual pleasures, and so on, things in which the physical body took an active part. In a higher type, in which the consciousness is working more in the mental vehicle, the pictures in the astral body will draw more of its attention; these pictures are shaped in the astral body by the vibrations coming outwards from the mental, and are perceived as pictures by the con-sciousness as it withdraws itself more into the mental body as its immediate vehicle. As this process goes on, and the more awakened consciousness responds to vibrations initiated from outside on the astral plane by astral objects, these objects grow "real," and become distinguishable from the memories, the pictures in the astral body caused by the re-actions from consciousness.

Let us note, in passing, that with the memory of an object goes hand in hand a picture of the renewal of the keener experience of the object by physical contact, and this we call anticipation; and the more complete the memory of an event the more complete is this anticipation. So that the memory will sometimes even cause in the physical body the re-actions which normally accompany the contact with the external object, and we may savour in anticipation pleasures which are not within present reach of the body. Thus the anticipation of savoury food will cause "the mouth to water." This fact will again appear, when we reach the completion of our theory of memory.

Now, having noted the changes in the vehicles which arise from impacts from the external world, the response to these as changes of consciousness, the feebler vibrations produced in the vehicles by the reaction of consciousness, and the recognition of these again by consciousness as memories, let us come to the crux of the question: What is memory? The breaking up of the bodies between death and re-incarnation puts an end to their automatism, to their power of responding to vibrations similar to those already experienced; the responsive groups are dis-integrated, and all that remains as a seed for the future responses is stored within the permanent atoms; how feeble this is, as compared with the new automatisms imposed on the mass of the bodies by new experiences of the external, may be judged by the absence of any memory of past lives initiated in the vehicles themselves. In fact, all the permanent atoms can do is to answer more readily to vibrations of a kind similar to those previously experienced than to those that come to them for the first time. The memory of the cells, or of groups of cells, perishes at death, and cannot be said to be recoverable, as such. Where then is memory preserved?

The brief answer is: Memory is not a faculty, and is not preserved; it does not inhere in consciousness as a capacity, nor is any memory of events stored up in the individual consciousness. Every event is a present fact in the universe-consciousness, in the consciousness of the LOGOS; everything that occurs in His universe, past, present and future, is ever there in His all-embracing consciousness, in His "eternal NOW." From the beginning of the universe to its ending, from its dawn to its sunset, all is there, ever-present, existent. In that ocean of ideas, all IS; we, wandering in the ocean, touch fragments of its contents, and our response to the contact is our knowledge; having known, we can more readily again contact, and this repetition—when falling short of the contact of the outside sheath of the moment with the fragments occupying its own plane —is memory. All "memories" are recoverable, because all possibilities of image-producing vibrations are within the consciousness of the LOGOS, and we can share in that consciousness the more easily as we have previously shared more often similar vibrations; hence, the vibrations which have formed parts of our experience are more readily repeated by us than those we have never known, and here comes in the value of the permanent atoms; they thrill out again, on being stimulated, the vibrations previously performed, and out of all the possibilities of vibrations of the atoms and molecules of our bodies those sound out which answer to the note struck by the permanent atoms. The fact that we have been affected vibrationally and by changes of consciousness during the present life makes it easier for us to take out of the universal consciousness that of which we have already had experience in our own. Whether it be a memory in the present life, or one in a life long past, the method of recovery is the same. There is no memory save the ever-present consciousness of the LOGOS, in whom we literally live and move and have our being; and our memory is merely putting ourselves into touch with such parts of His consciousness as we have previously shared.

Hence, according to Pythagoras, all learning is remembrance, for it is the drawing from the consciousness of the LOGOS into that of the separated Self that which in our essential unity with Him is etern-

ally ours. On the plane where the unity overpowers
the separateness, we share His consciousness of our
universe; on the lower planes, where the separateness veils the unity, we are shut out therefrom by
our unevolved vehicles. It is the lack of responsive-
ness in these which hinders us, for we can only
know the planes through them. Therefore we cannot directly improve our memory; we can only
improve our general receptivity and power to reproduce, by rendering our bodies more sensitive,
while being careful not to go beyond their limit of
elasticity. Also we can "pay attention;" *i.e.*, we
can turn the awareness of consciousness, we can concentrate consciousness on that special part of the
consciousness of the Logos to which we desire to at-
tune ourselves. We need not thus distress ourselves
with calculations as to "how many angels can stand
on the point of a needle," how we can preserve in
a limited space the illimitable number of vibrations
experienced in many lives; for the whole of the
form-producing vibrations in the universe are ever-
present, and are available to be drawn upon by any
individual unit, and can be reached as, by evolution,
such a one experiences ever more and more.

Let us apply this to an event in our past life:
Some of the circumstances "remain in our memory,"
others are "forgotten." Really, the event exists

with all its surrounding circumstances, "remembered" and "forgotten" alike, in but one state, the memory of the LOGOS, the Universal Memory. Anyone who is able to place himself in touch with that memory can recover the whole circumstances as much as we can; *the events through which we have passed* are not ours, but form a part of the contents of His consciousness; and our sense of property in them is only due to the fact that we have previously vibrated to them, and therefore vibrate again to them more readily than if we contacted them for the first time.

We may, however, contact them with different sheaths at different times, living as we do under time and space conditions which vary with each sheath. The part of the consciousness of the LOGOS that we move through in our physical bodies is far more restricted than that we move through in our astral and mental bodies, and the contacts through a well-organised body are far more vivid than those through a less-organised one. Moreover, it must be remembered that the restriction of area is due to our vehicles only; faced by the complete event, physical, astral, mental, spiritual, our consciousness of it is limited within the range of the vehicles able to respond to it. We feel ourselves *to be* among the circumstances which surround the grossest vehicle we are acting in, and which thus touch it from "outside"; whereas we "remember" the circumstances which we contact with the finer vehicles, these transmitting the vibrations to the grosser vehicle, which is thus touched from "within."

The test of objectivity that we apply to circumstances "present" or "remembered" is that of the "common sense." If others around us see as we see, hear as we hear, we regard the circumstances as objective; if they do not, if they are unconscious of that of which we are conscious, we regard the circumstances as subjective. But this test of objectivity is only valid for those who are active in the same sheaths; if one person is working in the physical body and another in the physical and the astral, the things objective to the man in the astral body cannot affect the man in the physical body, and he will declare them to be subjective hallucinations. The "common sense" can only work in similar bodies; it will give similar results when all are in physical bodies, all in astral, or all in mental. For the "common sense" is merely the thought-forms of the Logos on each plane, conditioning each embodied consciousness, and enabling it to respond by certain changes to certain vibrations in its vehicles. It is by no means confined to the physical plane, but the average humanity at the present stage of evolu-

tion has not sufficiently unfolded the indwelling consciousness for them to exercise any "common sense"
on the astral and mental planes. "Common sense"
is an eloquent testimony to the oneness of our indwelling lives: we see all things around us on the
physical plane in the same way, because our apparently separate consciousnesses are all really part of
the one consciousness ensouling all forms. We all respond in the same general way, according to the
stage of our evolution, because we share the same
consciousness; and we are affected similarly by the
same things because the action and re-action between
them and ourselves is the interplay of one life in
varied forms.

Recovery of anything by memory, then, is due to
the ever-existence of everything in the consciousness of the LOGOS, and He has imposed upon us the
limitations of time and space in order that we may,
by practice, be able to respond swiftly by changes
of consciousness to the vibrations caused in our
vehicles by vibrations coming from other vehicles
similarly ensouled by consciousness; thus only can
we gradually learn to distinguish precisely and
clearly; contacting things successively—that is, being
in time—and contacting them in relative directions
in regard to ourselves and to each other—that is,
being in space—we gradually unfolded to the state

in which we can recognise all simultaneously and each everywhere—that is, out of time and space.

As we pass through countless happenings in life, we find that we do not keep in touch with all through which we have passed; there is a very limited power of response in our physical vehicle, and hence numerous experiences drop out of its purview. In trance, we can recover these, and they are said to emergè from the sub-conscious. Truly they remain ever unchanging in the Universal Consciousness, and as we pass by them we become aware of them, because the very limited light of consciousness, shrouded in the physical vehicle, falls upon them, and they disappear as we pass on; but as the area covered by that same light shining through the astral vehicle is larger, they again appear when we are in trance — that is in the astral vehicle, free from the physical; they have not come and gone and come back again, but the light of our consciousness in the physical vehicle had passed on, and so we saw them not, and the more extended light in the astral vehicle enables us to see them again. As Bhagavân Dâs has well said:

If a spectator wandered unrestingly through the halls of a vast museum, a great art gallery, at the dead of night, with a single small lamp in one hand, each of the natural objects, the pictured scenes, the statues, the portraits, would be illumined by that lamp, in succession, for a single moment, while all the rest were in darkness, and after that single moment, would itself fall into darkness again. Let there now be not one but countless such spectators, as many in endless number as the objects in sight within the place, each spectator meandering in and out incessantly through the great crowd of all the others, each lamp bringing momentarily into light one object and for only that spectator who holds that lamp. This immense and unmoving building is the rockbound ideation of the changeless Absolute. Each lamp-carrying spectator out of the countless crowd is one line of consciousness out of the pseudo-infinite lines of such, that make up the totality of the one universal consciousness. Each coming into light of each object is its patency, is an experience of the Jîva; each falling into darkness is its lapse into the latent. From the standpoint of the objects themselves, or of the universal consciousness, there is no latency, nor patency. From that of the lines of consciousness, there is.*

As vehicle after vehicle comes into fuller working, the area of light extends, and the consciousness can turn its attention to any one part of the area and observe closely the objects therein included. Thus, when the consciousness can function freely on the astral plane, and is aware of its surroundings there, it can see much that on the physical plane is "past" —or "future," if they be things to which in the "past" it has learned to respond. Things outside the area of light coming through the vehicle of the astral body will be within the area of that which streams from the subtler mental vehicle. When the causal body is the vehicle, the "memory of past lives" is recoverable, the causal body vibrating more readily to events to which it has before vibrated, and

* "The Science of Peace."

the light shining through it embracing a far larger area and illuminating scenes long "past"—those scenes being really no more past than the scenes of the present, but occupying a different spot in time and space. The lower vehicles, which have not previously vibrated to these events, cannot readily directly contact them and answer to them; that belongs to the causal body, the relatively permanent vehicle. But when this body answers to them, the vibrations from it readily run downwards, and may be reproduced in the mental, astral and physical bodies.

The phrase is used above, as to consciousness, that "it can turn its attention to any one part of the area, and observe closely the objects therein included." This "turning of the attention" corresponds very closely in consciousness to what we should call focussing the eye in the physical body. If we watch the action taking place in the muscles of the eye when we look first at a near and then at a distant object, or *vice versâ*, we shall be conscious of a slight movement, and this constriction or relaxation causes a slight compression or the reverse in the lenses of the eye. It is an automatic action now, quite instinctive, but it has only become so by practice; a baby does not focus his eye, nor judge distance. He grasps as readily at a candle on the other side of the room as at one within his reach, and only slowly learns to know what is beyond his reach. The effort to see clearly leads to the focussing of the eye, and presently it becomes automatic. The objects for which the eye is focussed are within the field of clear vision, and the rest are vaguely seen. So, also, the consciousness is clearly aware of that to which its attention is turned; other things remain vague, "out of focus."

A man gradually learns to thus turn his attention to things long past, as we measure time. The causal body is put into touch with them, and the vibrations are then transmitted to the lower bodies. The presence of a more advanced student will help a less advanced, because when the astral body of the former has been made to vibrate responsively to long past events, thus creating an astral picture of them, the astral body of the younger student can more readily reproduce these vibrations and thus also "see." But even when a man has learned to put himself into touch with his past, and through his own with that of others connected with it, he will find it more difficult to turn his attention effectively to scenes with which he has had no connection; and when that is mastered, he will still find it difficult to put himself into touch with scenes outside the experiences of his recent past; for instance,

if he wishes to visit the moon, and by accustomed
methods launches himself in that direction, he will
find himself bombarded by a hail of unaccustomed
vibrations to which he cannot respond, and will need
to fall back on his inherent divine power to answer
to anything which can affect his vehicles. If he
seeks to go yet further, to another planetary chain,
he will find a barrier he cannot overleap, the Ring
Pass-not of his own Planetary Logos.

We thus begin to understand what is meant by
the statements that people at a certain grade of evolution can reach this or that part of the kosmos;
they can put themselves into touch with the consciousness of the LOGOS outside the limitations imposed by their material vehicles on the less evolved.
These vehicles, being composed of matter modified
by the action of the Planetary Logos of the chain
to which they belong, cannot respond to the vibrations of the matter differently modified; and the
student must be able to use his âtmic body before
he can contact the Universal Memory beyond the
limits of his own chain.

Such is the theory of Memory which I present for
the consideration of theosophical students. It ap-
plies equally to the small memories and forgettings
of every-day life as to the vast reaches alluded to
in the above paragraph. For there is nothing small
or great to the LOGOS, and when we are performing

the smallest act of memory, we are as much putting ourselves into touch with the omnipresence and omniscience of the LOGOS, as when we are recalling a far-off past. There is no "far-off," and no "near." All are equally present at all times and in all spaces; the difficulty is with our vehicles, and not with that all-embracing changeless Life. All becomes more and more intelligible and more peace-giving as we think of that Consciousness, in which is no "before" and no "after," no "past" and no "future." We begin to feel that these things are but the illusions, the limitations, imposed upon us by our own sheaths, necessary until our powers are evolved and at our service. We live unconsciously in this mightly Consciousness in which everything is eternally present, and we dimly feel that if we could live consciously in that Eternal there were peace. I know of nothing than can more give to the events of life their true proportion than this idea of a Consciousness in which everything is present from the beginning in which indeed there is no beginning and no ending. We learn that there is nothing terrible and nothing which is more than relatively sorrowful; and in that lesson is the beginning of a true peace, which in due course shall brighten into joy.

Clairvoyance and Mental Healing

Lecture delivered in Steinway Hall, Chicago, and reported in "The Progressive Thinker."

When Theosophy was first proclaimed in the modern world, a friendly Theosophical Society was founded in order to train people in the knowledge of Theosophical truths. It came to the world as an explainer, an expounder and a harmoniser of the many current opinions, of all those various thoughts and conflicting theories which existed alike in the world of science and the world of religion.

Somewhat misconstruing our work, we have tended rather to criticise the opinions of our neighbors, instead of trying to see the truth that was in them, and by bringing that truth to light acting as harmonisers between one cause and another. But just in as far as we have antagonised any form of thought, just so far as we have raised dissension and introduced bitterness into discussion, in so far we have been forced from our mission, for our mission is essentially that of peace bringing. The society does not seek to tear any man away from the opinions that he holds, but rather to show the place of those opinions in the world of thought, and to take up every school of philosophical, religious or scientific thought, and show just the place that it occupies in relation to others, considering each expression of thought as one channel of truth, and regarding these various channels as complementary, not as being antagonistic.

The position is one, of course, which it is often difficult to maintain, because everyone is fond of putting forth his own opinions in his own way, and quite naturally, perhaps, thinks his own way the best of all. None the less is it the task of the Theosophist to check that tendency to narrowness, to watch himself so that he shall not be betrayed into what may be called a sectarian defence of truth; but, recognising to the full that we are all extremely small vessels for truth, that we are all exceedingly narrow channels of the truth, and that the truth itself is a vast ocean—always much of it remaining which does not come down our particular little channels and pipes—our true attitude must be to recognise to the full the value of any truth that comes to our brothers, and to try to recognise the unity of the source, however much the different expressions may vary.

To-night I have chosen as my subject a class of ideas which give rise in our own time to a great deal of conflict—to schools of thought that are for the most part in antagonism, one against the other, so that if you look over the world of thought you will find different schools that are really closely allied but that are arrayed against each other as though they were enemies, and you find continually sub-divisions—each one a little different in its name, and each one particular body objecting, as it were, to the form in which the truth is presented by some other body, from whom it is divided by what is not essential but is a matter of detail. So that we have bodies that are called, for instance, Mental Scientists and Christian Scientists, and others who deal with mesmeric healing, and others who speak of themselves as Scientific Clairvoyants, and others again who speak of themselves sometimes as Mesmeric Clairvoyants, and all kinds and sorts of names, each one describing a small body that holds itself apart from all others.

Now, it is above all things important that the Theosophical Society give a hearty and fraternal welcome to all alike; that it shall not in any fashion put itself against any one of these forms of thinking; that it shall recognise the truth that is in every one of them; that it shall sympathise with the expression of that truth, and then shall utilise any knowl-

edge it may possess in order to harmonise one school
with another and to understand the view which each
school may take as to the truths of which it is the
particular exponent; and that is what I am really
going to try and do to-night. I am going to take
up some of those views, and try and show you their
place in relation to other truths; to show you how,
in the Theosophical teachings, these different views
have their places; how very often each school is an
exponent of part of a law; and that the recognition
of the whole of the law would be healthful both to
that school and to others who partially agree with it.
I am going to try and show you that looking at
these things from a Theosophical standpoint, we get
an illuminating truth thrown over the whole field of
thought; that we are able to explain apparently con-
tradictory opinions; that we are able to find the
place for thoughts that appear to be in antagonism
to each other; that the antagonisms arise because
they are fragmentary, and disappear when the connecting links are shown to exist. So that, really,
looking at the thing as a whole, we can see that here
this particular school is expressing its portion of the
truth, there that school has hold of a most valuable
fact in nature; here we find a group of people who
are bringing out a thought that has been left out
of sight by other schools, and again we find others
who are taking up a most important side of a natural

law and are laying stress upon it and drawing to it public attention.

Looking at things in this harmonious way, we find that the tendency of modern thought is to advance to a common goal, and that divergent as the stream may appear, although sometimes they may look as though they were flowing in antagonism to one another, these little antagonistic turns are only partial and temporary. They are all flowing to a common sea, and they are carrying those who follow that course in the same direction and towards the same ultimate goal, and that goal is a recognition that spirit is the ruling force of the universe, and that matter is only the expression taken and used in order that spiritual forces may express themselves on different planes and in different regions; that fundamentally all energy comes forth from God; that as that energy works in one region or another it takes a different veil of matter, and therefore shows a different phenomenal appearance. But we know that' looking at these forces we shall find that they are all gradations of the one, and that what is essential is the recognition that the force moulds the matter, not that the matter gives birth to the force; that is, that the Universe is the Divine Thought in expression, that everything that exists is the Divine Idea taking shape as phenomena, and that instead of looking at the universe as a soulless piece of mechanism working with inflexible mechanical rigidity, we are to recognise it as the living thought of a living consciousness, as in every way flexible and under the influx of that thought, as being continually changed and modified as the thought comes into fuller and fuller expression; and that as the more we realise that and live it, the swifter is the evolution of the whole, the nearer is it to the fulfilling of the Divine purpose in manifestation; that this is the goal towards which thought is tending.

We have scientific thought which studies phenomena, and gradually by a study of the phenomena is, as it were, compelled to a recognition of the forces underlying them. Thus we notice that in modern science all the great triumphs are now being made in a region where forces are recognised before matter is inferred—an extraordinary change of position. In the past matter was studied, and the presence of force was implied. Now the forces are asserting themselves, and by the action of the forces matter is argued for, inferred from, the presence of the forces. And you will realise exactly what I mean by that abstract statement, if you consider that in all the latter discoveries electricity has played so great a part, and that ether has been accepted as a necessary hypothesis, not because it is observed as matter, but because its existence is necessary to explain the workings of the forces; that is, that matter is inferred because the force is observed —just the reverse of the earlier tendency of science, when the force was rather grudgingly recognised as made necessary by the observations of the material forms. Now it looks as though science were going more and more along that line; as though science were plunging more and more rapidly into the realm of forces; and as though we were going to discover sub-divisions of matter because of the differences of vibration that are measured in connection with forces.

Let me recall to your memory what I have mentioned here before—the vibrations that have been classified lately by Sir William Crookes. Those are vibrations in ether, and they include all sounds, all vibrations of heat, of light, all vibrations of electricity, whether slow or rapid. They include certain unknown vibrations that are mathematically argued to exist but have not yet been proved, and they include the Röntgen rays, enormous as is the rate of their vibration. Then again, there is an inference of vibrations yet more rapid than those which have most lately been added to the knowledge of the scientific world.

The result of this is that science is beginning very doubtfully to admit the possibilities of the varieties of ether—that is, there is no longer going to be a single kind of substance inferred, but varieties of

ether will be wanted in order to explain the difference of the rates of vibration—thus coming exactly
on to the lines of the Theosophical teaching that in
the physical world matter exists in seven different
conditions; the solid, the liquid, the gaseous, three
kinds of ether, and then protyle—the original physical material out of which every physical combination is built up.

Science is very rapidly approaching that conception, and it is in connection with these varieties of
ether that the questions of all the lower forms of
clairvoyance arise. In order to understand clairvoyance we have to distinguish between the different
stages. All of us possess normal sight, and that
only means that we have certain cells which are
modified so that parts of the cells vibrate in answer
to ethereal vibrations that fall between two limits
of speed. All the vibrations by which we see are
comprised within narrow limits. Those which give
us the sense of red, those which give us the sense
of violet, are the extremes of our vision.

Now the eyes of some human beings, as you probably know, are trained to such an extent that within
the limits of the spectrum they can see a great many
more colours than you and I can see. If, for instance, we had present a Cashmerian weaver, he
would take a group of wools that you and I would
say were all the same colour, he would divide them

up, and sometimes a man will obtain twenty different shades of colour where you or I could only see one. We have not yet developed the power of sight to that fineness of vision which distinguishes these intermediate shades, merely because by physical heredity our eyes have not been trained along that line. For hundreds of generations Cashmerian weavers have been trained to distinguish the minutest shades of colour, and the wonderful softness that you get in Cashmere shawls, in Cashmere carpets and curtains, is simply due to the extraordinary eyesight of the Cashmerian weavers. They see differences where we see none, and the result is that they grade colours as none of us could possibly grade them, so that colour fades into colour by imperceptible modifications.

That is the first thing to recognise in connection with sight. The next thing to recognise is that we do not all see the same, even in regard to minuteness of vision in cennection with the violet rays that are the limit of our sight. Some people can see further than others in this, and that only means that they can vibrate a little faster. Then you come to the ultra-violet rays, which the normal eye, however highly developed, does not see, but the clairvoyants see them. There is no break; there is no gap in this, the vision getting finer and finer. An ordinary clairvoyant of the poorest description will see the ultra-violet rays, and it does not need very much to enable anyone to see these rays, just a little development of a centre in the brain which responds to more delicate vibrations of the ether than our eyes are able to respond to.

So we may get grade after grade in clairvoyance, until we come to those who are able to see by the vibrations that are known as the X-rays. That means, for instance, that a clairvoyant would be able to see through this board. Placing a book on the other side of the board, the clairvoyant would read it. Place a book or a key, anything you like, the other side of the board, and your Röntgen rays will enable you to see it. Now, of course, we know that that is done by apparatus. The clairvoyant can see by means of those vibrations directly, without any methods introduced by apparatus; and so we get a class of people, who with their ordinary eyes, as it is thought—but not really by their eyes, but by the use of a centre within the brain thrown into vibration by these rays—can see an object using those rays as you and I can see, using the vibrations that we call light.

Now, anybody can do this if he is mesmerised. Anyone of you if mesmerised would become a clairvoyant. You all possess the power, but everyone has not developed it to the point where, without mesmerism, he is able to use it.

What is it mesmerism does? It simply makes you vibrate at a little higher rate than you normally vibrate. It is nothing more than a current of magnetism, which is thrown from one person to another, and sets ˙the ether in the patient's body vibrating. When that ether is made to vibrate by this external stimulus, it vibrates all through the brain as well as through the rest of the body. It brings into momentary activity a centre in the brain which is normally inactive, and by means of that centre the subject becomes clairvoyant. So in a vast number of experiments, a person mesmerised has been made to diagnose an obscure disease; being thrown into the hypnotic trance he cán see the body of the patient, and state exactly the condition of the internal organs; and there is many a doctor now, who when he is puzzled by a disease, will simply mesmerize a sensitive person and then utilize this clairvoyant power in order to guide him in his treatment of the disease. As science understands this, clairvoyance will be brought in more and more in order to assist in medical science; until, after a time, this will be as normal a way of looking into disease as the very clumsy methods of observation at present employed, the greater number of which depend on inference rather than direct observation.

Let me go on to another form of clairvoyance which is sometimes a little puzzling. If you get out of health you will sometimes become temporarily clairvoyant. If your nerves are strained, if you are under the stress of great trouble, great anxiety; if you have lost a very dear friend and are suffering keenly; any of these conditions may make you clairvoyant for a time; and it is under these conditions that people sometimes see the outer form of a friend who has passed away. Sometimes it is simply in the world of ether; sometimes it goes on to what we call the astral world, or the intermediate state—that state in which the soul is for a time, between leaving the physical world and entering on the heavenly existence.

Let me give you an instance of this, rather peculiar, but valuable clairvoyance; because it was a Materialist who saw—a person who did not believe in the soul, who did not believe that anything survived when the body perished, and for that reason it was the more interesting, inasmuch as the imagination did not come into play, being against the whole tendency of thought of my friend. The woman was a Materialist in her philosophy. She lost a friend who was very dear to her, between whom and herself there existed a strong magnetic sympathy—a sympathy so strong that while the friend was in the body anything that strongly affected her affected also the Materialist. Suppose, for instance, that the friend was ill, then our Materialist would feel depressed and unhappy. If the friend was in trouble then the Materialist would always know it by a sense of trouble in herself. When the friend died our Materialist was almost broken-hearted, and the result on the physical health was extreme. For some weeks after the death of her friend she saw the form of that friend under very peculiar conditions. She saw the decaying etheric double of her friend, not the astral form; she did not come into contact with the soul that had passed out; she simply came into contact with the ethereal part of the physical body, that which is most readily seen by a very slight tension of the nervous system. She actually saw, day after day, the process of decay; one of the most painful instances that I ever came across in a very wide experience of these abnormal occurences; for, with all her disbelief in anything existing, she was literally haunted by the decaying image, seeing the etheric double decaying stage by stage, with the perishing of the dense physical body. And such a phenomenon may recur over and over again, in any case where the mind is fixed entirely on a friend as expressed only in a physical body—a very slight intensification of the nervous system may make visible what is normally hidden—the gradual decay of the ethereal part of that body, which tends very often to be drawn by magnetic affinity towards anyone who has been tenderly attached to the person during physical life.

A higher form of clairvoyance is that of the astral world. ·Then things may be seen at a distance; then friends may be communicated with thousands and thousands of miles away, and most of you would be able to develop at ·least partial astral clairvoyance if you were in the habit of practising what is called thought-transference; if you were in the habit of trying to bring your minds into harmony to communicate with some one at a distance. By doing that you would organise your astral vision, and you might without very much difficulty see your distant friend, and so come into close magnetic relations, although thousands of miles might separate you from that friend. The method of doing it most of you probably know. You begin by an active act of the imagination. You think strongly of your friend's outer appearance. The effect of that is that the thoughts work in thought matter and make an image of your friend in the mental world which, animated by and vibrating to your thought, draws to itself astral matter which builds the astral form. The astral form being in existence, only a little magnetic action is needed to render that form visible even to a slightly developed physical sight; and that is perhaps one of the easiest experiments in which, without any danger, the power of astral clairvoyance may be developed. There is one very curious way that it may be developed, that I will mention to you, because science is going to discover this very soon, and it is sometimes well to realise how very closely science is on the track of those (at present) abnormal powers.

There is a form of clairvoyance connected with ether which is very easily developed, and its action is exactly similar to the action of the telephone. Supposing that in your own brain you set up vibrations which enable you, as it were, to realise very strongly the face of a friend. Some of you can visualise, as it is technically called. Every artist can do it. That is, by effort of thought you can really see your friend's face. You can so clearly realise it that it becomes almost as though you were looking at a picture. How many of you, if you were to try to do this, would find that you were able to get a picture of your friend so that you could really see it, although not, of course, with the physical eye? Now, when you have made such a picture, it has produced in your brain a likeness in ether. It is only vibrations. You have set up vibrations in the ether; these go out from you just like a shell. Probably most of you know how sound and light vibrations go out; and if you have seen an account of what are now called Marconi's waves, you will notice there are some pictures representing vibrations and that they go out like a number of concentric shells, just like the ripples in water that you get if you throw a stone into it: you see the ripples go out from the centre in every direction, circular ripples. Well, that is exactly what happens when you set up an electric vibration in the ether—electric ripples go out in circles all round you into space, and when you make an etheric picture of a friend's face those vibrations go out into space. When they are in space you cannot call them a picture, they are only vibrations; but let them be received by a similar instrument to the one that started them, and they will produce in that a similar picture to the one with which they started. Take your telephone—the voice vibrations do not go; no sound travels along the telephone wire. All that travels are the electric vibrations, and those, as they come into contact with the other disk, make the disk vibrate, and it is the vibrations of the disk that give out the words and reproduce the voice of your friend.

In the same way, by electric vibrations, a picture has been transmitted. I have no doubt that you have seen an electric instrument, or read about it, by which a picture could be made at the other end of an electric wire, so that a picture produced in one town could be reproduced in another simply by the electric current. If you can do that by an electric current and two machines, the generator and the receiver; if you find by Marconi's experiments that you can do the same thing without a communicating wire at all, because the vibrations go out in shell-like fashion through the ether; is it so very difficult to realise that, inasmuch as every thought that you think is a vibration, it causes an electric vibration in your own brain; that those electric vibrations in the brain, caused by your thought, can pass through ether, and reaching a brain attuned to your own by sympathy, reproduce the vibration in that brain, and the brain by its own action, like the disk of the telephone, will give the picture, which the thought originally produced?

That is the rationale of thought transference. It is not your thought picture, friends; it is the vibrations connected with that picture; and when those come to a sympathetic brain, it is there that the picture is reproduced. It is not that the picture travels through space; it is the vibration that travels through space and the picture form belongs to the brains at the two ends—the brain that originates and the brain that receives.

The thought forms that I spoke of are different from these pictures. Those are again etheric vibrations, expressing particular thoughts and particular emotions; but they are symbolic in their character. One of the characteristics of these thought forms and of these desire forms is that they are generated

automatically—and those of you who have studied
dreams will understand something of the symbolism
in which the brain is always working and realise the
translation which occurs—the brain being a trans-
lating instrument with which every one of us is endowed.

This leads us on to the very interesting question of
mental healing, for it all turns on thought vibrations. The mental healer will tell you practically
that he can heal a disease by thought; that he does
not want drugs; that he does not even see the patient. You will find plenty of mental healers who
are able to heal at a distance. There are hundreds
and thousands of cases in this country and in other
countries where a well-trained mental healer, in answer sometimes to a telegram, will cure a case of
disease without coming into physical contact with the
patient at all. I have known a number of such
cases, and certainly every mental healer will be able
to mention numbers through his or her own experiences. But what I want you to realise is how it is
done.

The mental healer, as a rule, simply asserts the
power of mind over matter—a true assertion. He
will say, Mind is the controlling force. Make the
thought right and the body will have to follow.
Make the thought pure and the body will be in
health. Identify yourself with mind and your body

will follow suit. This is carried so far by some schools of healers that they actually assert that there is no evil, there is no pain; that there is no disease, there is no suffering; and some of them cure by that assertion.

In some schools, for instance, in curing disease the healer will instruct the patient to say: "I am not suffering, I am not in pain, I am well, and I am not diseased," and by the reiteration of that thought produce the healthy condition. That is one form of healing that probably many of you will be familiar with. Others do not go so far as to say there is no pain; that is they do not deny the pain; they do not deny the disease; but they say: "Recognise that you yourself are that which does not suffer, which is not diseased, and from yourself, which cannot suffer or be diseased, can proceed nothing which will permit a material disturbance." By these means cures are often effected. Let us further recognise that sometimes the very reverse is brought about from that which is desired; that sometimes a physical disease disappears and a more subtle disease makes its appearance; that sometimes a bodily suffering vanishes and a mental suffering takes its place; that in some cases, while the disease has vanished, absolute mental injury has asserted itself and partial attacks of insanity have resulted; and if we want to understand we must take the whole of these into consideration. All these things occur. I recognise the cures and understand their mode; and I want, if I can, to put before you the theory rather more clearly in detail.

It is true that the mind can cure disease. It is true that the action of the mind can either kill or cure and can either wound or heal. Science justifies that statement now in the mesmeric and hypnotic experiments that have been made; for many a wound has been produced by mesmeric suggestion; many a cure of paralysis has been made by hypnotic suggestion. Both curing and injuring have been done when the person has been entranced and the suggestion has been made. More than that, it is not necessary that any words should be used, for mental suggestion is quite enough. Any person can produce a result on the hypnotised patient by thinking clearly what he means to effect. He can produce a wound; he can produce paralysis; he can produce absence of pain and presence of pain; he can remove a nervous affection or he can impose that nervous affection at his will. Science admits this now to the full, and the essentials of mental science are endorsed really by physical science at the present time, and that is a matter that ought never to be forgotten, for all these mesmeric and hypnotic investigations have confirmed to the full the basis of mental healing.

Now let us take up the rationale of the healing. Suppose, for instance, that a person is suffering from a wound in the arm. The mental healer is going to heal that wound. How? Some would say, "Oh, we could not do that. We cannot cure a physical lesion; we can cure many forms of disease, but we cannot cure absolute lesion." That is not correct, because it can be cured if you know how to do it. There are two great principles in mental healing. This is where the Theosophical understanding of the fundamental principle may perhaps help some of our friends who have been looking at the question partially rather than fundamentally. For there are two great lines of mental healing. One of them depends on expelling from the physical body any substance which is inharmonious with the body as a whole. That deals with one class of disease. Another class of disease—many separate diseases come under each—depends on inharmonious vibrations between the astral, the etheric and the dense part of the physical body. You have got your vibrations jangled, instead of rhythmic and harmonious. Under that come all nervous diseases; under that a large number of digestive troubles; under that the very many diseases arises from disturbance of circulation, and so on. These all come under one great head, lack of harmony in the vibrations that go on in your body, whether in the dense or in the etheric part,

or even in the astral. Another class altogether is a
disorganisation of tissues; and these are, as a rule,
not much dealt with by mental healers.

Now, let us take the first class that I mentioned,
where you have something that you need to expel.
You have a foreign substance present in the human
body which does not vibrate harmoniously; you
have matter which does not build up properly into
that body, and you have to get rid of it. How
shall you do it? First you need to recognise its presence and exactly where it is. Then yon need to set
up vibrations by your thought which will affect first
the astral and then the etheric, and lastly the physical, and those vibrations being in harmony with the
key-note of the vibrations of the body of your patient, will throw out of that body everything inharmonious wit it. Then you must know the key-note to
which your patient vibrates. That is what Keely is
struggling after on the physical plane. That is
what Keeley is beginning to discover from the physical standpoint. The mental healer approaches it
from the mental standpoint. But the difficulty is
to find what we call the key-note of the patient;
and you must have, in order to discover that, knowledge which goes deeper than the mere assertion of
the power of mind over matter. You have got to develop the powers of your own soul, and when the
soul is active you can find the vibratory note to

which your patient responds, and until you do you are working haphazard; you are working without understanding exactly what you are doing; and on the mental plane you are just like the physician who experiments with his drugs—he is not quite sure of the effect, but he hopes the drug will turn out all right. If it does not and the patient dies—well, it is unfortunate, but he could not help it. If it does, he has more knowledge to help him in treating cases. I am afraid a good deal of mental healing is rather of that nature and character—the healer does not know exactly how to work, and he simply tries to set up good vibrations, hoping that those good vibrations will work out the effect that he desires.

Now take the commoner class, where you simply have to regularise. It is in this that most of the successes take place, because all that is wanted is to begin harmonious vibrations in the mind; get your patient to think harmoniously, peacefully, restfully, and then you will gradually, from the mind of your patient, set up vibrations that will pass down through the astral to the physical and harmonise the whole. All that is wanted for that is the power of concentaration, and the power of will; but that is a good deal, and the reason that so many people fail in mental healing is because they do not get their minds steady so as to send down steady vibrations. Unless you can fix your mind on that one point, and steadily from that point start perfectly quiet, steady vibrations you cannot cure disease; and the success of the mental healer depends upon concentration and then on the power of the patient to reproduce the vibrations set up from this quiet centre. If you want to do it for yourself, take a quiet time; sit down quietly where no one disturbs you; fix your mind on a high ideal; think some great spiritual thought; shut all the world away and let the mind grow quiet and still. Under these conditions, when all is quiet, set up the vibration of health, which is harmony, and in that way you will harmonise the whole vibrations of the body and soul, and gradually, without any risk of danger; expel the disease, as you may say, that is bringing the jangling vibrations into rhythmic and harmonious working.

Let us now come to that other class where actual lesion occurs and where there is lack of material present and you want to deal with that. Suppose you have a bad strain; suppose you have a wound; suppose you have a nerve which is becoming atrophied; and you want to heal those. There is only one way of doing that effectually, and it needs pure thought and physiological knowledge. First you want to know what that tissue looks like in its healthy state so that you can make a picture of it as it ought to be. That is the first stage of such healing—you must know how it ought to be. If, for instance, it is a wound you must be able to know how that muscle ought to appear if it were healthy; and, to know that, you require clairvoyance, for you must be able to see the corresponding muscle in a healthy state of the patient's body. As all people differ in detail, what you want is to use the symmetry of nature to help you in your healing work. For this class of healing, then, clairvoyance is an absolute necessity. You must be able to see what it ought to be in the healthy state; and the way you do it is to look at the corresponding muscle which is uninjured, and the corresponding nerve which is uninjured, and observe its exact state. You then proceed to make in your own thought a mental picture of the healthy condition. You then project that healthy picture in the brain of your patient, producing that healthy picture in his brain. The vibrations set up by that are guided down the nervous road, as it were, the nerves cross the place where the injury occurs, and you build up, first in astral matter, a perfect picture of the healthy muscle or nerve. Then you build into that etheric part, and then the body itself builds in the dense particles which are wanted for the restoration of the muscle to health. You must supply the model; nature herself then builds into that model. And that is why so few cures of this kind are done—people do not

really know how to do it. They do not realize these
stages—the making of the healthy picture, which is
like a model at first, just as though it were a model
of sand shaped out of a mould, and then, the metal
being poured in, takes the form of the mould. You
make the matrix or mould of the healthy condition,
and then nature, in her normal working, builds the
material particles into the matrix you have supplied. In that way the wound is healed, or the
nerve is nourished, atrophy ceases, and the nerve or
the muscle is cured again.

These, as I say, are the most difficult cases, but
they are well within the reach of mental science, the
moment the mental scientist understands the law
with which he is working and trains his own mind
in that fixity and concentration without which the
mental processes cannot effect a cure.

You see, then, how theosophical study proves and
illuminates what you may call this practical work;
how it brings a more complete theory in order to
give that knowledge which is necessary for the
thorough utilising of these higher powers.

. Supposing anyone of you desires to use those powers, the first thing you have to do, before trying to
use them, is to purify your own life and your own
thought. If mental healers are not pure in life and
in thought, if they are simply the ordinary men and
women sharing in the ordinary weaknesses and frail-

ties of commonplace humanity, they transfer their own conditions to their patients while they are conferring the bodily healing. There is where the danger of the whole practice comes in. Suppose that your mental healer has thoughts that are not thoroughly pure, these thoughts will be transmitted to you while you are being cured of your bodily disease, and your mind will be demoralised while your body is being cured. The result is that poison is being poured into the cause while you are only healing the effects; you will be continually sowing fresh seeds of disease at the very time that you are removting those which have grown up into a plant.

If, then, you are going to resort to a mental healer, choose your healer. Be careful whom you admit to that close relationship, to your inner life, for you are no longer dealing with the physical; you are dealing with the mental plane and you must be very careful what influences you on that plane, and that you do not buy the health of the body by the injury or the poison of the mind.

You will realise, then, why Theosophists speak so much about care; why they so insist that before any one develops these powers he shall develop purity of character, nobility of life, compassion and tenderness of thought; why they put the development of the soul before the development of powers; why they try to lead their pupils to develop these

inner forces before they use them on the outer plane,
before they use them in connection with their fellow-men.   It is not that we challenge facts; it is
not that we do not realise the powers; but we also
realise their far-reaching effect, and we know that
to be a mental healer, in the real sense, a man
should be a saint at the same time; and the higher
the power is that he utilises, the cleaner should be
the hands that he brings to the divine work.   All
that were called the miracles of the saints were but
the workings of natural law, the bringing of spiritual powers down to the physical plane—still loftier
powers than the mental powers, more potent, more
tremendous in their scope.   Therefore, side by side
with the healing of physical disease by the adept,
there is always the reference to the sin which is in
touch with the physical disease.   Only as sins disappear can physical health be secured; only as the
inner self is purified can the outer self be thoroughly
healthy.

We are going onwards to a humanity where disease shall be unknown; where pure bodies shall be
the tabernacles of pure minds; within these the temples of the living God.   The pure body, the pure
mind, the manifested presence of the Deity—these
are the stages of human evolution, of that ideal humanity towards which we are evolving at the present
day.

How vital, then, that we understand the forces that are coming more and more into manifestation. How vital that by careful study we should realise the presence of these forces and understand the method of their working. But above all, let the spirit of love, of compassion, of sympathy, of brotherhood, be the motive power that shall underlie the utilisation of all these forces in the world. As we become possessors of them let us use them for human good. As we find that they come into our hands, let us utilise them in order to lift up humanity, to raise it spiritually, intellectually and physically at the same time. Let us realise that the raising power is from above, not from below; that pure minds are the things we should search after; pure bodies will come as a necessary result. Therefore let us keep the proportion, let us keep the balance—have more of the mind than the body, more of moral evolution than of physical, more of purity than of physical health. To put it in the words of a divine teacher, "Seek first the Kingdom of God and His righteousness, and all these things shall be added unto you." But if you seek first the lower things, forgetting the higher, then you will often stumble and fall, even in grasping after the lower. Seek the highest; the lowest will inevitably come into your hands; and your joy shall be in the realisation of your oneness with the Divine rather than in your power over the manifestation of physical nature.

www.ingramcontent.com/pod-product-compliance
Lightning Source LLC
Chambersburg PA
CBHW050803270326
41926CB00025B/4521